Praise for *What We Say Matters*

"*What We Say Matters* shows how speech can be a spiritual practice. A language of the heart has the power to create a world of connection, peace, and compassion in our own lives and in the whole human family. I am excited and inspired by how Judith and Ike present the NVC principles from the context of yoga philosophy and Buddhism in a way that is simple, clear, and practical, yet filled with depth and wisdom. I highly and enthusiastically recommend this book."

—John Kinyon, trainer and mediator, The Center for Nonviolent Communication

"As a longtime student of NVC (thanks to Judith and Ike), I am grateful for the clarity and wisdom of the material presented in *What We Say Matters*. I was inspired and encouraged by their personal stories and am excited to experiment with the practical suggestions and exercises. When I imagine the people who will read and use this book, I feel hopeful that we can all contribute to creating a more peaceful world."

—Marcia Miller, co-owner of Yoga on High, Columbus, OH

"When I read Judith and Ike's book, I feel happy, as though I have friends who speak to me and for me (rather than *at* me or *down* to me) and who will coach and counsel me through the intricacies of communicating more clearly and carefully, heart to heart, so that we may flower in each other's presence. Thank you for this offering, a treasure that helps me to unfold inside."

—Edward Brown, Zen teacher, author of *The Tassajara Bread Book* and *The Complete Tassajara Cookbook*

"This book reminds me of conversations around the dinner table at Judith and Ike's house, exploring ways to deepen our consciousness and more fully live this one precious life. Now everyone is invited to be at that table."

—Kit Miller, Director/Celebrator, Bay Area Nonviolent Communication

WHAT WE SAY MATTERS

BY JUDITH HANSON LASATER

Published by Shambhala

Restore and Rebalance

Relax and Renew

Yoga Abs

Living Your Yoga

A Year of Living Your Yoga

30 Essential Yoga Poses

Yogabody

Yoga for Pregnancy

Yoga Myths

Teaching Yoga with Intention

BY JUDITH HANSON LASATER AND IKE K. LASATER

Published by Shambhala

What We Say Matters

BY IKE K. LASATER

Published by PuddleDancer Press

Words That Work in Business

WHAT WE SAY MATTERS

Practicing Nonviolent Communication

REVISED EDITION

Judith Hanson Lasater, PhD, PT

Ike K. Lasater, JD, MCP

SHAMBHALA

Shambhala Publications, Inc.
2129 13th Street
Boulder, Colorado 80302
www.shambhala.com

This edition published 2022. The updated edition includes
a new preface and a completely revised chapter 8.

Cover & interior design: Kate E. White

9 8 7 6 5 4 3 2 1
Second editon

Printed in the United States of America

Shambhala Publications makes every
effort to print on acid-free, recycled paper.
Shambhala Publications is distributed worldwide by
Penguin Random House, Inc., and its subsidiaries.

ISBN: 978-1-64547-104-2
Library of Congress Control Number: 2022013193

CATALOGING-IN-PUBLICATION DATA IS AVAILABLE
FROM THE LIBRARY OF CONGRESS

For our children and their loved ones

CONTENTS

A new idea is first condemned as ridiculous,
and then dismissed as trivial, until finally
it becomes what everybody knows.

—WILLIAM JAMES

PREFACE

WHEN SHAMBHALA PUBLICATIONS released *What We Say Matters* in 2009, I was unsure how it would be received. At the time I was known as the author of instructional books about yoga practice, yoga philosophy, and anatomy and kinesiology as they applied to yoga teaching. But *What We Say Matters* was a different endeavor altogether: It was a book about communication. And not just about communication per se, but communication as a transformational and self-awareness tool. As it turns out, all my concerns were unfounded.

Happily, many yoga students and teachers around the world have embraced the book and let me know how much it has helped them in their life. I was, and am, humbly grateful to hear this.

Verbal communication is practically the definition of what it means to be human. Language can unite us or divide us; it can stir us to war or make us collapse in laughter. Best of all, verbal communication can open new worlds of knowledge to us. Language can be used to help us know ourselves better. It can help give us the freedom and awareness to choose new ways of being in the world, which directly contributes to our and others' happiness.

In fact, our words change the world every time we speak. They certainly have the potential to change our personal world, but they also can change the larger world. This is because our words not only have the power to affect the people immediately around us but also have the power to affect people we will never meet when our words are indirectly passed on to others.

Marshall Rosenberg, the creator of Nonviolent Communication, stated, "My words reflect my thoughts, my thoughts reflect my beliefs, and my beliefs run my world, especially the unacknowledged ones." This sounds very similar to Buddha's "Do not seek enlightenment; merely cease to cherish beliefs."

I find it interesting that both Buddha and Rosenberg do not expect us to give up our beliefs. Rather, both implore us to notice how our beliefs can habitually narrow perception so that we only have one way to see the world: our way.

What We Say Matters attempts to offer our readers a way to make speech first about this self-awareness and then about empathy for self and others. When we choose to bring these qualities into our daily lives, into our family relationships, or into our teaching of yoga, everything changes. We feel more connected to ourselves and those closest to us.

It is my fervent hope that this book both challenges you and supports you as you learn NVC. Enjoy the revised chapter 8. Take the exercises to heart, and try to practice them a little every day.

But most of all, do not lose heart. The process of learning NVC is so much more than just learning "which words to say." NVC actually starts with us becoming clear about the background intention that forms the impetus for us to speak in the first place. In fact, it could be said that using NVC begins with *communicating with ourselves internally before we open our mouth to attempt communication with others.*

Finally, Nonviolent Communication is the process of letting go of the communication patterns that keep us tied to unsatisfying conversations and unsatisfying relationships and contribute to our dissatisfaction with many life situations.

My deepest wish is that you take this book to heart and begin to gradually change how you approach communication. I predict you will like the results. But even better, as you integrate NVC into your life I hope it becomes easier to live, communicate, and share from your deepest Self.

Namaste,
Judith Hanson Lasater
San Francisco, CA

ACKNOWLEDGMENTS

WE WISH TO THANK the people who inspired us, taught us, and supported us as we wrote this book. Marshall Rosenberg, PhD, was the catalyst who helped us to see how *satya* and right speech could be lived, as we observed his practice and teaching of Nonviolent Communication. Our three children and our daughter-in-law have all given us great reason to become more aware of speech and how we could use it to create connection and clarity in our relationships. Finally, we wish to acknowledge all of our teachers, including B. K. S. Iyengar and Charlotte Joko Beck. To all of these people, we are humbly grateful.

Judith wishes to thank her yoga students and her friend and Zen teacher, Linda Cutts Weintrab, for their constancy. Ike would like to thank his teachers and colleagues on the road to incorporating the skills and understanding of Nonviolent Communication into his day-to-day life.

In particular, he wants to thank John Kinyon for his support and companionship in the adventure of learning to mediate using NVC and learning how to offer trainings for others to do the same. We both thank Julie Stiles for her keen eye, sensitive review, and helpful editing in the writing stages of this book, and special appreciation for her collaboration with Ike in the creation of chapter 9.

We also thank our publishers, Donald Moyer and Linda Cogozzo, for their vision and for their practical help as this book took shape.

INTRODUCTION: WHY WE WROTE THIS BOOK

Speech is a mirror of the soul:
as a man speaks, so is he.
— PUBLILIUS SYRUS

"THAT'S NOT A FEELING," my husband Ike stated, gazing at me across the kitchen with a mixture of excitement and smugness. My look back at him was less than pleased. He had just returned from a seminar with Marshall Rosenberg on Nonviolent Communication (NVC), and he was telling me that my words did not describe "feelings" according to what he had learned. Unfortunately I was unable to hear his excitement or appreciate his insight, because I was too busy reacting negatively to him "telling me how to talk."

When we tell this story at the NVC seminars that we teach together, we offer it as a perfect example of how not to practice the principles we share in this book. But the difficulty we had with each other was nothing compared with what happened as we began to "use" this technique with our three teenagers. We laugh now, but it was a painful period, as first Ike and then I began to change something we thought we already knew how to do: communicate.

Speech is the most human of activities. Babies begin making sounds from birth to communicate their needs, and a child's first word is a cause for celebration. Speech allows for the functioning of society on all levels. It would seem that nothing could be more natural than the use of speech to express our needs and to respond to the needs of others.

But belying its simple appearance, speech is actually created out of a complex interplay of factors. Our thoughts, beliefs, and perceptions powerfully shape our language to reflect our particular world. Without a clear awareness of our words, we can be dumbfounded daily by interactions that result in the opposite of what we intended. Research tells us that only a small percentage of what we say is actually heard, and even less of that is actually understood. Add to this the fact that different languages express actions and thoughts with different structures, and it is a wonder we understand each other at all.

Our interest in communication began much earlier than that incident in the kitchen in 1997. We both began to study yoga in 1970 and learned about the eight limbs, or *ashtanga* principles, of the yoga philosophy presented by Patanjali in the Yoga Sutra. The first principle for the practice of yoga is called *yama*, meaning "restraint." There are five restraints, the first and most important of which is *ahimsa*, or nonviolence. Another yama is *satya*, or truth. The practitioner is admonished to speak the truth or, more accurately, to restrain from speech that is not true.

Ike and I both found that this ancient advice to speak the truth raised many questions. Whose truth? Don't we all experience reality differently? In the book *Life Strategies*, Phillip McGraw states, "There is no reality, only perception." Ike and I found that while we agreed with truth as a value, we were not as easily able to understand it as a practice, as something we did with each utterance.

Throughout the years, we also became interested in Buddhist meditation and took up a daily practice of sitting in the Zen tradition. As with yoga philosophy, we found that Buddhism offered us a list of precepts, one of which is "right speech," or using speech in a way that does not harm oneself or others—very much like satya. Again, we agreed in principle but were a little baffled about how to practice it, other than to consciously not tell lies.

One day at a Buddhist retreat, Ike was almost casually introduced to the basic principles of Nonviolent Communication and, in the way of so many things, before long he found himself in a workshop with Dr. Rosenberg, the founder of the method. Soon I joined Ike in the study of NVC. All I remember of the first couple of years was that I didn't get it at all. We both just tried to focus on the most basic structures from the technique, and slowly, over time, we began to integrate the work into our lives. What helped us most was simply practice. Lots of practice.

We organized a regular weekly practice group at our house and tried to practice with each other every day at home. We joked that we lived in an "NVC ashram." We took seminars, some as long as ten days, to immerse ourselves in NVC. And we finally realized that what we were doing was learning a foreign language, the language of empathy and compassion.

We found an interesting interplay between the conscious practice of meditation and yoga asana and the conscious choice of words. Dr. Rosenberg's approach felt familiar to us, as we attempted to bring our practices off the meditation cushion and yoga mat and into our lives as spouses, parents, teachers, and citizens.

The thesis of this book is that what we say matters—that is, when we speak, we change the world. Blending the spiritual awareness of the power of speech into the actualizing technique of Nonviolent Communication creates a powerful tool for affecting not only our lives and the lives of those around us but also the world at large. Without awareness of the power of our language, we continue to reinforce the patterns, both emotional and psychological, that contribute to our suffering and the suffering of others.

Using speech as a spiritual practice is the act and art of bringing a deeper awareness to our words so they not only connect us with ourselves but also reflect what is truly alive in us. When we do this, we help create the kind of world we want to live in and leave to future generations, because then our words promote life.

We now know that learning NVC needn't be so difficult. We finally feel that we are beginning to understand satya and right speech in ways we never thought possible. It has taken us years to understand that the first thing that must happen if we are to practice spiritual speech is an internal shift in awareness. From that initial shift, our language then begins to shift without conscious effort to reflect on the outside what has already happened inside. When these two shifts occur, we are more likely to enjoy our interactions with others.

We wrote *What We Say Matters* to share with you what we learned about how to approach this work. The book is organized into nine chapters. We begin by discussing satya, right speech, and NVC itself. Then we explore the principles of NVC in how we talk to ourselves, our partners, our children and parents, and at the workplace. Each chapter includes practices intended to help you take NCV deeply into your life. To help you do so, consider:

- keeping a journal of specific phrases or sentences that have helped or not helped you connect with yourself and others, or of your other practice experiences;
- asking a friend to be your empathy buddy, to help you approach a difficult conversation;
- forming a weekly *What We Say Matters* study group.

Our continued learning has created effects that have been nothing short of miraculous in our lives. We are so happy you are joining us in this adventure. We hope that some of these techniques will help you speak in a way that meets your needs for clarity and ease and the world's need for compassion.

1

SATYA AND RIGHT SPEECH

Is sloppiness in speech caused by ignorance or apathy? I don't know and I don't care.

—WILLIAM SAFIRE

THE ANCIENT TEACHINGS of yoga and Buddhism have many things in common. They both evolved from the Hindu culture, they both contain techniques that teach us how to live a life of fulfillment free from suffering, and they both offer teachings specifically about speech and its importance in our lives.

The Yoga Sutra of Patanjali, the ancient sourcebook delineating the psychology and practice of yoga, offers two *sutra* (verses) on the subject of speech. The first is in chapter (or *pada*) II, verse 30. Here Patanjali lists the five *yamas*, or restraints, that are recommended for the practitioner of yoga. These restraints are *ahimsa* (nonharming), *satya* (truth), *asteya* (nonstealing), *brahmacharya* (chastity), and *aparigraha* (nongreed). The second mention of satya is in pada II, verse 36. Georg Feuerstein translates this (in *The Yoga-Sutra of Patanjali*): "When grounded in truthfulness, action (and its) fruition depend (on him)." This means that as we practice satya on deeper and deeper levels, whatever we say is an accurate reflection of reality. This verse could also mean that when we are grounded in the state of yoga, the state of pure being, then we cannot say anything that is not the truth, and so anything we say is true. It is not true because we have made something come true, but rather because there is no separation between our consciousness, the truth, and what we speak.

There are, however, other aspects to the practice of truth. All yamas, including satya, are considered to be secondary to the expression of ahimsa, or nonharming. I (Judith) understand that we can never "tell the truth" if we ignore the foundational practice of nonharming.

In the Yoga Sutra, satya is offered in the context of a restraint. This means that we are to consciously hold back speech that will be harmful. It is thus implied that we remain aware of all speech, so that words that are not truthful, and therefore harmful, are avoided. Importantly, no instruction is given in the Yoga Sutra about what we are to say or how we are to speak. Instead, Patanjali exhorts the practitioner about what to avoid.

The Buddhist eightfold path offers teachings similar to those found in yoga. The eight practices are divided into three sections. The first section is about wisdom and includes right understanding and right thought. The second section is about ethical conduct and includes right speech, right action, and right livelihood. The final section is about mental discipline and includes right effort, right mindfulness, and right concentration.

Right speech is speech that furthers the practice of the speaker and contributes to the well-being of others and the world. Right speech is therefore intentional speech that rejects mindless chatter, gossip, slander, and lies. When we are honest with ourselves, self-reflection often reveals that much of our speech is harmful at worst and unnecessary at best.

The practice of right speech is just as difficult to apply as the practice of satya. Both teachings describe what to do, but neither gives much guidance on how to do it. Additionally, there is no way to measure if one has "done" right speech or satya. I can know when I have practiced the *asana* (posture) of Salamba Sirsasana (Headstand), but whether I have practiced right speech or satya is pure judgment.

Nonviolent Communication can thus be a boon to practitioners of satya or right speech. The techniques of NVC are first and most importantly about inner awareness. Then NVC offers specific ways to consider and practice speech. Like yoga and Buddhism, NVC considers speech to be very powerful. This power is twofold.

First, there is power in paying attention to how I phrase what I say. The way I phrase a thought to myself before I speak expresses how I think and what I believe about the world. One of my favorite sayings is: My words reflect my thoughts, my thoughts reflect my beliefs, and my beliefs, especially the unexamined ones, run my world.

To consider this in the opposite way, whatever unexamined thoughts I have are going to shape how I act and how I interact with others. They will determine how others see me and how they treat me. For example, if I tell myself through my thoughts that I am worthless, I will begin to act that way, and others will treat me as if that were the truth.

The heart of any spiritual practice begins with remembering at all times to be present with my inner states. This remembrance is crucial, because it is the foundation for understanding this important teaching: *I am not my thoughts*. I have thoughts, but they are a manifestation of my being and are not who I am. One of the best ways to remember that I am not my thoughts is to cultivate the habit of being present first with myself and then with my speech, both internal and external. The way I say things reifies my beliefs, especially the belief that I am my thoughts.

An example of this is that we sometimes say the opposite of what we mean. I might feel hurt because you did not arrive for our date on time. But instead of saying that, I say, "I guess you don't care about our relationship." This statement is not likely to get me the connection I want, and it might even start a fight.

The second way speech is powerful is that what we say changes the world. That is not an exaggeration. How we express ourselves affects not only what we think but if and how that speech connects us to the other. We advocate using speech to connect first to yourself, then to the person you are with, and finally to the task at hand. Most of us have been taught to connect first with the task at hand, then with the other person, and finally with ourselves.

But unless we are connected with ourselves, with our feelings and needs, then our speech will not clearly reflect what is true for us. It will also distort our relationship with others and the world. We will act out of this distortion, which will contribute to our suffering and the suffering of others. Both yoga and Buddhist practices are centered on learning to bypass the creation of this suffering.

Here is an example of how words contribute to suffering. One person is at home, waiting for the other to arrive at the agreed-upon time of 7 p.m. When the arrival occurs at a later time, it is not uncommon for the person who was waiting to say something like, "Where in the heck were you? Why were you so late?" It is likely that the waiting person is feeling uneasy or afraid or concerned, but instead of that, they express anger and irritation. It is also likely that the person who arrived after the agreed-upon time will respond with irritation and anger as well, and now the two are off to the races, talking about who was at fault instead of dealing with the feelings and needs of both parties. This sort of conversation creates suffering.

Nonviolent Communication is a learnable technique that can teach us how to put the values of right speech and satya into practice, so we can use speech to deepen our spiritual practice and carry that practice into a heartfelt connection with others. We begin to learn this technique in the next chapter.

2

NONVIOLENT COMMUNICATION

The three most important mantras are:
Tell the truth. Tell the truth. Tell the truth.
—JUDITH HANSON LASATER

THE FIRST TIME I (Judith) took a seminar on Nonviolent Communication from Marshall Rosenberg, I spent a lot of time squirming in my seat. It wasn't that I didn't like what he was saying; it was that I couldn't understand how to do it myself.

As Dr. Rosenberg had conversations with various people in the workshop, one by one they would laugh, cry, or both, as they felt the power of connection with him. "How does he do that?" I thought. It seemed like he was working magic. I couldn't begin to explain what he was doing; I just knew I wanted to be able to use my words in the same compassionate way. Years later, with more training under my belt, I have a deeper understanding of how NVC can be a practical application of satya and right speech.

In the early stages of learning NVC, it can seem to be all about word order and choice—syntax—and in this book we focus most of our attention on these aspects. But bear in mind that NVC is fundamentally about *intention.* Syntax is just a strategy to remind us of our intention.

The underlying intention in using NVC is to connect: to connect with ourselves first and only then to attempt to connect with others. Out of this connection, we can create mutually satisfying outcomes. The words we use will change, based on the situation or subculture in which we find ourselves. Therefore we hope you will use words that have both meaning and resonance for the person you are talking with.

The practice of being connected with yourself in a visceral, noncognitive way is powerful. We are unlikely to connect to another human being unless we are connected with our own needs. This is not something most of us are taught as children, and generally it takes time and practice to develop the skill. In fact, as children we are sometimes actually taught to deny our own needs.

Have you ever heard a parent tell a young child, "No, you don't want that vase," as the curious child reaches for Grandmother's precious art piece? The statement is not true; the child definitely wants the vase in order to fulfill a need for learning or perhaps for fun. The child is actually being told, "You can't touch the vase." From these little life experiences, we are being taught that what we think we want is not really what we want. No wonder then that when we are forty-five years old and sitting in an NVC seminar, we are flummoxed and confused when someone asks us to identify our needs.

As part of the conditioning process, as we lose touch with our own needs, we learn to protect ourselves from criticism, avoid punishment, and redirect blame. Learning to connect at the level of needs is a way of learning to step out of our habitual ways of reacting. As you identify, time and time again, what needs were and were not met by your actions in a situation, particularly one where you reacted habitually, the possibility opens up to act differently in the future. In this way, you can use NVC to change how you relate to yourself and others.

When you make it a practice to connect with your needs, you shift into learning mode. For example, your coworker is complaining again that your boss never listens to anyone. You could ignore his comment or agree with it, or you could silently translate his statement into an expression of his own needs. Perhaps he wants to be seen or heard or appreciated. Once I hear my coworker's statement as a statement of his needs instead of as a statement about someone else, I notice a different reaction in myself. I then have the opportunity to respond directly to his needs instead of responding from my reaction. If you do find yourself reacting instead of responding, you might inquire into the need you were seeking to meet by your reaction, as well as what needs of yours were not met by the interaction.

The natural result of this inquiry is the question, How might I do it differently next time, in order to better meet my needs? We encourage you to do this inquiry without a sense of judgment, punishment, blame, shame, self-condemnation, or guilt. Just simply inquire about what needs were and were not met and what might be ways to better meet them. Thus inquiry, which is at the heart of the practices of yoga and Buddhist meditation, can be brought into our daily interactions and activities.

When you practice this inquiry, you learn to become aware. You mourn and celebrate your conduct, building from what you liked and shifting away from what you didn't like, all in order to better meet your needs. Soon you begin to remember, when you are in a moment of agitation, to try a new choice. Then you learn from that choice. The natural consequence of this process is that you learn skills that are in alignment with meeting your needs and the needs of others.

Thus, from our perspective, at the core of NVC is not only developing the skills and practicing them but also gaining experience in choosing new possibilities based on needs, instead of repeating habitual patterns. By being connected with our own needs, our intention is clarified moment by moment. This is speech as a spiritual practice.

AN NVC PRIMER: THE BASIC CONCEPTS

There are four basic steps in learning to use NVC. These steps are meant to be used not as a formula but as a launching pad. Holding tightly to these four steps can disconnect you from the present moment and can stand in the way of clear and true communication. So start with these four steps, but be willing to move beyond them as you feel more at home with the process.

Step 1: Make observations. To make an observation is to report on what we commonly call the facts. The Yoga Sutra calls this *pramana* (pada I, v. 7). Some observations are: "The month is August" or "John arrived at noon."

"John arrived late" is not an observation; it is a judgment. Why? Because John may not believe that he is late, and if Mary tells him he is late, he might deny it and argue the contrary. Perhaps in John's belief system, ten or fifteen minutes is not really late, whereas Mary maintains that even one minute past the agreed-upon time is late. An observation would be: "John arrived ten minutes past the time Mary remembers him agreeing to arrive."

It is important to make this distinction because when we use judgments in our conversations with others, we tend to get off track and begin arguing about what is true—in this case, whether or not John was late. Such an argument probably will not get to the heart of how John and Mary would like to be together. What might be true is that Mary was worried about John's safety, while John was happy that he was feeling so relaxed about this time with Mary. Instead of enjoying each other, they might spend their time together at odds with each other.

That John was late or not late is what I (Judith) call a pseudo fact—a judgment masquerading as a fact. Some common pseudo facts are "You are driving too fast" or "It is really cold in here" or "That was a really good movie." I call these pseudo facts because at first these statements sound like simple observations, but in fact they are not. In Thomas Byrom's translation of *The Dhammapada*, Buddha is quoted as saying, "Do not seek enlightenment; merely cease to cherish beliefs." Our opinions and beliefs are pseudo facts. A pseudo fact is "It's hot in this room." It is asserted as a fact, but it is indeed a judgment. Another person could say, "No, it's not. I'm cold." An observation would be (looking at a thermometer): "It's 80 degrees in this room." This statement is not likely to become the crux of an argument.

Imagine the following. A parent knocks and enters the bedroom of a teenager with the following words: "This room is a mess. Please clean it up by tomorrow morning because company is coming." We almost guarantee that the response from the teenager will be: "It's not a mess." If the parent persists, the teenager will likely switch to, "But I like it this way." And if that fails, the teenager will resort to the time-honored, "Whose room is it anyway?" We would bet lots of money that what follows from these interchanges is not a period of sweet connection between parent and child.

A more desirable connection is likely to result if the interchange begins with observation language. Pay attention to how different you feel when you imagine the communication starting with, "When I see your clothes on the floor, dishes with food on them on your desk, and your bed unmade . . ." The key point here is to notice the difference between making an observation and making a judgment. For example, to say, "When I see that your room is a mess . . ." is not to make an observation. The term "mess" is a judgment; messes are not desirable. (More on the teenage bedroom drama to come.)

Observation used in this way is an expression of what we call spiritual speech. It is learning to leave out our judgments and beliefs *about* what is observed and just describe it as a camera would record it. Later in this chapter, we offer practice exercises to help you to refine your awareness of observations versus judgments.

We are not proposing a new set of rights and wrongs. It is not wrong to use judgments. We just want you to be aware of using them, so you can learn what ensues from using judgments and what ensues from using observations instead. Then the choice is yours.

The judgments at issue here are moralistic opinions about someone or something being right or wrong. We will never be able to do away with evaluating whether our needs are being met or not. That is a form of judgment. But in making that evaluation, we are not condemning anyone for their motives.

Step 2: Name your feelings. Feelings are emotions and are connected to bodily sensations. Feelings are constantly changing and constantly arising. They tell us simply whether our needs have been met or unmet in that moment. In that sense, feelings are "flares" from the unconscious that alert us to the state of our needs: met or unmet.

For example, we might feel happy, content, at ease, connected to self and others, or full of energy. These feelings tell us that we are perceiving that our needs are being met in that moment. Or we might feel sad, lonely, afraid, irritated, or confused. These feelings tell us that we are interpreting and therefore believing that our needs are not being met in the moment.

All human beings have feelings, and they are constantly arising and changing. If you don't believe that, get married and have kids! Feelings are signals shooting from the depths of the unconscious mind, alerting us that we need to pay attention. In that way, feelings are like a yoga pose. When we bend forward in Uttanasana (Standing Forward Bend) and feel lots of stretch in the hamstring muscles at the back of the upper thigh, attention is immediately brought there. The sensation is telling us to pay attention to the hamstrings and how they need some release. This act of paying attention is the practice. Spiritual practice is not the asana but the act of noticing during the practice of the asana. Part of the benefit of a regular asana practice is to remind us to pay attention. Feelings serve the same purpose.

If we learn the habit of paying attention to feelings as they arise, we are immediately brought into the present moment. And this is the hallmark of spiritual practice. You cannot simultaneously be paying attention to your feelings and be lost in thoughts about the situation. Being lost in thoughts is our suffering.

One important thing to remember is that, according to the NVC model, feelings arise separately from what other people say and do. Others might stimulate my feelings, but my feelings are mine and are unique to how I experience the world. One person might feel sad from hearing something on the news, while another might feel happy upon hearing the same thing. The difference lies in the individual, not in the news. The news does not create feelings, although it may very well stimulate feelings. There is a difference.

Let's say that you and I go to a movie. You cry during the movie and I don't. The observation is that we both saw a movie. The stimulus was the same for both of us. We reacted differently, based upon our unique makeup. Our makeup comes with us from the womb and is shaped by our life experiences, particularly the patterns formed in early childhood.

Another thing to remember is that to say, "I feel like you are a pain in the neck" is not to express a feeling. What is being stated is an opinion. Many people use the word "feeling" to express beliefs, thoughts, and images. To say, "I feel like you were acting unfairly" is not expressing a feeling; it is analyzing how you acted. If instead you said, "When I heard what you said to me, I felt sad," you would be using observation language ("When I heard what you said") followed by feeling language ("I felt sad"). This use of language brings the speaker back to her own truth. It is what occurs when we observe thoughts arising in meditation. We predict that you will enjoy the responses you receive when you do not mix the expression of feelings with analysis or opinion.

Finally, remember that "feelings" as used in NVC do not include those that involve another person. For example, "I feel abandoned" involves another person. It takes another person to abandon me. Instead I could say, "I feel lonely and afraid." Those feelings may have arisen when the other person left.

Try saying these two sentences out loud. First, "You abandoned me." That expresses a belief about someone's behavior. Upon hearing that sentence, the other person may feel that he is being judged. He may even say, "I didn't abandon you," and you might respond with, "Oh, yes you did," and an argument could ensue. Now say aloud, "When you left the house, I felt lonely and afraid." The other person cannot argue with your feelings of being lonely and afraid, because they are yours and are alive in you. In that sense, they are real to you. It would not sound strange to hear someone say, "No, I did not abandon you." But it would sound very strange to hear, "No, you are not feeling lonely and afraid." It simply does not make sense.

Step 3: Express your needs. This phrase puts some people off because they equate needs with being "needy." But needs in NVC are what arise naturally when life expresses itself. We all have needs to survive (air, water, food, shelter) and needs to thrive (touch, play, intimacy, sexual expression, creativity). We all have a need for respect and a need for our autonomy to be recognized. We also have spiritual needs, such as for peace, or wholeness, or connection with Deity. Dozens of human needs have been identified. Needs are simply life expressing itself, and they are held by all human beings. When we are in touch with our needs, we are in touch with life itself as it arises in us.

Maybe that is why we find babies so fascinating and dear. Babies are always in touch with their needs. When they are hungry, wet, or bored, they let us know immediately. And babies do not resent their needs or perceive them to be a burden on their parents. As adults we often sublimate our needs or give up on getting them met because of judgments like, "I shouldn't have this need" or "No one would give me what I need anyway."

When our needs are unmet, our fundamental humanness is denied, and when that happens, we cannot be fully human, fully happy, or fully healthy. Learning to identify our needs and how to get them met is a fundamental life skill that is part of what it means to practice spiritual speech.

Sometimes Marshall Rosenberg, in his public workshops, draws upon the work of economist Manfred Max-Neef, who presents a list of nine universal human needs: affection, creation, freedom, identity, participation, protection, recreation, subsistence, and understanding. You may find that using just these nine needs is an excellent place to start your practice of NVC; identify these needs when they arise in you.

I (Judith) once met a Rolls Royce salesman at a party. He told me that no one "needs" a Rolls Royce, and that it is his job to convince them that they do. In a few words, he summed up the basis of our consumer culture. A car is not a need but a strategy for getting a need met. What might be the need in this case? Perhaps it is for sustenance to support a family or for ease of movement when meeting commitments. The salient point is that those needs can be met by other cars, other means of transportation, other methods of getting around.

We run into trouble when we confuse strategies with needs. Most of us do this all time. We think the need is to get into a specific university or to get a certain job or to learn a certain yoga pose. But these are all strategies for getting our needs met. In the cases listed above, can you guess what the needs might be? Perhaps getting into a particular university might be a strategy for meeting a need for safety or identity. Getting a certain job might be meeting a need for community or creativity or (financial) security. And mastering a certain yoga pose might meet a need for fun or meaning or physical well-being.

Separating needs from strategies is critical in relationships. When a couple argues, it is often over strategies. For example, a couple might be arguing over where to go on vacation. One wants the beach, and the other wants the mountains. It seems like they can come to no resolution. From the point of view of NVC, this argument is about strategies. It is likely that each person has the same needs: rest and recreation. They have just chosen different strategies for meeting those needs. When the couple focuses on the needs first, the strategies often work themselves out in a mutually agreeable way.

Love is an interesting part of the needs inventory. Many people would call love a feeling, but NVC suggests that love is a need. If I have the strategy for getting love from a specific person and that person does not give it, I am stuck without getting my need for love met. But there are always many strategies for getting any particular need met, and so it is with love. I can get love from many other sources in my life. Viewing love as a need frees me up to search for another strategy to get that need met.

If we look in on the situation we visited earlier, it might go something like this: "When I see your unmade bed and the clothes on the floor of your room, I feel frustrated, because my needs for order and beauty are not met." I am being clear that the teenager's room is not the problem. Instead, by discussing the situation in this manner, I am making it clear that what is stimulating my reaction of frustration is *what is arising in me.* True, the state of the room is the stimulus for the feelings. But when I make an observation in this manner, it becomes clear that my needs are what is being discussed. The other person's actions or nonactions are not the cause of those feelings.

Step 4: Make a request. When I make a request, I am trying to get my needs met in that moment. Requests may seem like the easiest part of the model to understand, but actually they are more difficult to make clearly than you might think.

Requests have the following characteristics: They are made about the present, and they are doable. Requests in the NVC system are about a specific action to be done in the present. An example would be, "Are you willing to make your bed within the next five minutes?" or "Are you willing to tell me now when you might be willing to make your bed?"

It would not be a request to ask, "Would you show me that you love me?" The problem is that it is not doable. How would either person in the conversation know that the "showing love" request had been met? Showing love is not something a camera could take a picture of. A doable request might be reworded as, "Would you be willing to hug me now?" or "Would you be willing to sit on the couch now and listen to me tell you about my day for five minutes without saying anything?" These sentences are requests because not only are they referencing the present, but they ask for something that can actually be done, and in a sense measured, by the parties involved. Both people would know when the request had been met.

A request does not ask for something in the future like, "Will you wash the car tomorrow?" No one knows what they are going to do tomorrow. Instead we could ask, "Are you willing to commit now to washing the car tomorrow afternoon?" or "Are you presently willing to meet on Saturday for ten minutes to decide which health insurer we are going to use?"

The important distinction to understand when learning requests is the difference between a request and a demand. Often the only way you know when you are making a demand instead of a request is by what you do (or think of doing) when the other person says no to your request.

If you make a "perfect" request using the new phrasing you have learned and the other person still says no, and if you then respond by trying to pressure them into agreeing, you made a demand rather than a request. The sweet tone and kind face you use when asking does not make it a request. The expectation of having your request met is not in the spirit of spiritual speech. When we have an unspoken demand, it is about power. To make a true request, we need to remain open to the outcome and open to allowing the other person to say no. (Later we discuss the next step you can take to get your needs met if your initial request is denied.)

So finally, adding a request to the scenario taking place in the teenager's room, it might sound like this: "When I see your unmade bed and the clothes on the floor of your room, I feel frustrated because my needs for order and beauty are not met. Would you spend ten minutes with me now, making the bed and picking up the clothes off the floor and hanging them in the closet?" This phrase makes a specific request; it also reveals that the request is about the needs of the speaker, which makes it more likely that the hearer will be willing to comply.

The syntax you learn in NVC is designed to help you uncover your intention—for example, the intention of connection with the other person—and remembering it in the moment. I (Ike) have found, for myself and in working with others, that using the basic sentence of NVC verbatim can be extremely valuable as you are learning this new language. We call this the "training wheels" sentence:

"When I hear _____, I feel _____, because I need _____; would you be willing to_____?"

My experience is that people who skip this step take longer to learn NVC, or they might never really integrate a "needs" consciousness. Using the training wheels sentence over and over ingrains the basic distinctions that are so important to Nonviolent Communication: distinctions between observations and judgments, between feelings and evaluations masquerading as feelings, between needs and strategies, and between requests and demands. These distinctions are embedded in the structure of the training wheels sentence, so using the sentence prompts awareness of them. Practicing the training wheels sentence is the only way I have found to establish these basic distinctions at a deep level. The sentence encourages us to focus on each of the four parts of communication—formal observations, feelings, needs, and requests. Once these are fixed in your consciousness, then you can more easily use colloquial phrasing to create the connection between yourself and others that you are seeking. When you are firm in your intention of communicating based on getting your needs met, you might even use words that sound judgmental, yet you will be able to connect with others. People often wonder why, when they are using all the "right" words, they are not getting the results they expect. Perhaps it is because they are not yet clear in their intention. When you have the clear intention of connection, the words become the strategy to accomplish this. The particular words and their syntax become secondary.

The central precept of Nonviolent Communication is to focus on connection between yourself and others, and

THE FOUR COMPONENTS OF NONVIOLENT COMMUNICATION

1. **Observations**	vs.	Evaluation, judgment, interpretation, diagnosis
Attention, awareness, acceptance		Thinking about what happened, analysis
What happened, what is, facts		Moralistic judgment, right/wrong, good/bad
2. **Feelings**	vs.	Thoughts, beliefs, opinions, images
Emotion, body sensation		"I feel like/that . . ."
Feedback about our needs		"I feel abandoned/ rejected/betrayed . . ."
3. **Needs** (universality)	vs.	Strategies, concrete behavior (diversity)
Life in action, universal qualities		Action to meet needs
Language that connects to life energy		Specific to person, time, place
Internal experience independent of externals		Often cultural, habitual, conditioned
4. **Requests** (for action)	vs.	Demand (coercion/power over) and vague wants
Response given freely, willingly		Denial of choice: have to, should, must, can't
Requests as gifts of meeting needs		Use of fear, shame, guilt, obligation, duty
Clear present, positive, action language		Concept of deserving punishment or reward Use of vague, abstract, future language

out of that connection to fulfill your needs and the needs of others. We often believe that if we can analyze a situation clearly, we will be able to get what we want. NVC suggests that it is only when we are connected to our own needs and the needs of others that we can cooperate to meet the needs of everyone. The table on pages 34–35 identifies a number of basic feelings and needs, and might help you be more precise in expressing yourself.

PRACTICING NONVIOLENT COMMUNICATION

Observations

- Write down three judgments about others and three judgments about yourself that have arisen in your mind during the past week. Now translate those judgments into observations.
- Use observation language in three interactions every day for one week. Write these down and share them with an empathy buddy: a friend who would be willing to give you empathy, and vice versa. You can be available to each other as needed, or you can speak regularly, either in person or by phone.

Feelings

- For one week, at 9 a.m., 12 noon, 3 p.m., and 6 p.m., stop and note what you are feeling. Write it down.

- What feelings arise today when you believe you are right? Write them down.

Needs

- At 9 a.m., 12 noon, 3 p.m., and 6 p.m., stop and note what you are needing at that moment. Write it down. Remember, needs are universal, and they arise in us independently of others.
- Note mentally or write down three instances in the last few days where you expressed your "needs," but they were really strategies masquerading as needs.

Requests

- Think of a request you would like to make of three people. It can be the same request or three different ones. Write down these requests, refine them according to the principles of NVC, and then ask them. See what happens.
- Hear everything people say to you today as an expression of "please" or "thank you." Note how different you feel when you understand the words you hear as requests. In this case, the implied request the other is making of you is either "please meet my needs" or "thank you for meeting my needs." This is true regardless of the actual words used.

FEELINGS AND NEEDS

Feelings

Frustrated	**Sad**	**Scared**	**Overwhelmed**
impatient	lonely, heavy	terrified	shocked
irritable	hurt, pained	startled	exhausted
annoyed	brokenhearted	nervous	helpless
agitated	despairing	full of dread	listless
disgusted	sorrowful	desperate	tired

Confused	**Peaceful**	**Affectionate**	**Happy**
hesitant	calm	warm	glad
distressed	content	tender	excited
embarrassed	satisfied	appreciative	joyful
suspicious	relaxed	friendly	delighted
puzzled	quiet, still	loving	confident

Playful	**Interested**
energetic	inspired
expansive	intense
adventurous	curious
mischievous	surprised
alive, lively	fascinated

Needs

Well-Being	**Connection**	**Expression**
sustenance, nourishment	love, acceptance	celebration, play
safety, security, protection	to matter, be nurtured	to see, be seen
health, wellness	intimacy, friendship	authenticity, congruence
movement, recreation	respect, consideration	autonomy, freedom
rest	equality, communion	choice
balance, order	community, belonging	meaning
ease, flow	to know, be known	creativity
peace, harmony	cooperation, support	contribution
touch	presence, awareness	inspiration
growth, learning, efficacy	understanding, clarity	humor
wholeness	honesty, trust	passion
beauty	purpose	integrity
	power, influence	gratitude
	inclusion, mutuality	

3

FOUR COMMUNICATION CHOICES

A new idea is first condemned as ridiculous,
and then dismissed as trivial, until finally
it becomes what everybody knows.

—WILLIAM JAMES

SPIRITUAL SPEECH is a way of bringing the teachings of *satya* and right speech into everyday practice. Without a technique such as Nonviolent Communication, these values and ideals can remain just that. While we may value dearly the ideas of satya and right speech, how can we live them in a way that brings us home to ourselves and creates the kind of world we want to live in?

Often when we are first learning NVC, we think it is about the literal language or specific words we use. And while it is important to use the "training wheels" sentence presented in chapter 2, it is even more important to remember the primary point: Practicing NVC involves first and foremost an internal shift in awareness that allows us to use the specific language effectively. Remember, first value connecting with yourself and then allow your internal shift. Only then should you attempt to use NVC language. It is this internal shift of awareness and intention that allows speech to become a spiritual practice.

When we struggle with NVC language, it may be a sign that we have not yet made this internal shift. Use the skills you have learned in your yoga or meditation practice, or just slow down and notice what is going on inside you. Without this self-awareness, we forget that *what we say is always about ourselves*, especially about our feelings and needs, and is *never* about the other person, because whatever we say is coming out of our perception of what is. This is true even if the words we use sound like they are about or directed to the other person.

CHOICE 1: FOCUS ON SILENT SELF-EMPATHY

Starting with yourself is important, especially when you are learning. Most of us have been taught by culture and religion that focusing on ourselves is selfish and is always the worst choice. Nothing could be further from the truth. Unless and until we are aware of what we are feeling and needing, we are unlikely to relate in a direct way with others. Unless we are clear in ourselves, our words create consequences (karma) for everyone that we will probably not enjoy.

Our words live on through our relationships, and the effects of our words are passed down through the generations as "emotional DNA." Emotional DNA is just as powerful in shaping our lives as is the physical DNA we received from our ancestors. Emotional DNA creates the patterns of thinking, believing, and acting that control our lives. By using the tool of self-empathy to become aware of what is arising in us, we can begin to be clear about the patterns of speech we have inherited. We then have the choice born of awareness, and we can begin to use language in a way that heals ourselves, our children, and the world.

To practice self-empathy, sit or lie comfortably in a quiet place, and recall something someone said to you today that caused a reaction in you. You may want to write down the interchange, to slow it down in your mind. Once you have the situation in mind, distill it down to one simple sentence that the other said to you. Use observation language to start.

This means that you say to yourself, "When I remember Tom saying ______________ (make an observation), I feel ______________ (name the feeling that arises), because my need for ______________ is not met." Make sure your observation is exactly what the other person said or did and not your judgment of it. Stay away from words such as *messy, late, good, mean,* and *irritating;* they are judgments because they imply evaluation.

Try it several times, and experiment with different "feeling" words and different "need" words. When you find the words that are true, you will know it. Confirmation that you have hit upon something that is alive in you is often experienced as a strong physical reaction. It might be tears or a feeling of euphoria as you say the words to yourself.

Don't give up until you get some form of confirmation that is not just an intellectual awareness. This energetic shift is the manifestation that you have connected with your deepest self. You have given yourself empathy for what is alive in you. Life is now serving life. There is something healing about naming what is going on inside you.

Finally, another way you will know that you have connected with yourself is that you will notice a curiosity about the other person, about what might have been going on with them when the communication happened, or what might be going on with them now. Our advice is to persevere with silent self-empathy until this curiosity arises in you. It may take more than one session to arrive at this place of curiosity.

If you try to force yourself to be interested in what is alive in the other person before you are ready, thoughts may arise like, "I don't really care what that so-and-so is feeling or needing right now." If that happens, continue with your process of self-empathy until you can think of the other with an open heart and you feel compassion, or at least curiosity, arising in yourself for the other.

CHOICE 2: FOCUS ON SELF-EXPRESSION

The second communication choice is self-expression. This means that you state aloud to the other person what is going on with you. Again, use the training wheels sentence while you are learning: "When I heard you close the door with more force than I like, I felt irritated, because my need for respect and peace was not met." (Note the use of observation language: "with more force than I like" instead of "slammed." "Slammed" conveys a judgment that the other person can definitely argue with you about.) Do not fail to follow this self-expression with a clear, doable request. If you stop with the first sentence, the other person may very well begin to argue with you and say things like, "I didn't slam the door" or "you always say that" or "I can never do anything right for you, can I?" Without a doable request, people often hear the expression of observations, feelings, and needs as criticism. (You will follow your self-expression with an immediate request, detailed below.)

The whole interchange would then be: "When I heard you close the door with more force than I like, I felt irritated, because my need for respect and peace was not met. Would you tell me . . . ?" Here is where you make your request, which is detailed under the fourth communication choice. Make sure the whole interchange uses no more than thirty words. Using more words is likely to result in disconnection.

Remember, even if you make a request using "perfect" NVC language, the person may still hear criticism and judgment. If so, give yourself self-empathy again and try once more. Remember, NVC is a practice like yoga and meditation and therefore requires lots of repetition. Your intention is not to get it right but to connect with yourself and with the person in front of you. It is this connection that holds the potential for changing the world.

CHOICE 3: FOCUS ON GIVING EMPATHY

The third choice, either to begin or to continue your communication process, is to focus on giving the other person empathy. This can either be silent empathy in your own heart or empathy spoken out loud. When I (Judith) first learned about silent empathy, I was not impressed. I thought, How can what I think make any difference unless I actually tell the other person what I'm thinking?

Then I tried using silent empathy and was astounded by what happened. I learned that when I use silent empathy with the other person, a change happens. *But that change occurs in me.* This is so because, in order to empathize silently with the other person, I have to empathize with myself first. In the beginning of my practice of Nonviolent Communication, silent self-empathy could take minutes, hours, or days. Now, with practice, I can sometimes feel the shift that comes with self-empathy in a matter of seconds, and then I can choose to give empathy to the other almost immediately. I actually now experience self-empathy and empathy for the other as virtually the same process, like a continuum.

Silent empathy for the other person also causes a change in my expression and body language that the other person picks up. This shift is sometimes palpable between us, and invariably when I shift, the other person senses it and shifts as well. Ike and I are both continually amazed and pleased by how powerful it is to give the other person silent empathy.

To give silent empathy is to intuit or guess what the other person might be feeling or needing in the moment. Be sure to start with observation language. Your inner dialogue might go something like this: "When I heard her say ___________, I am guessing that she was feeling ___________ and needing ___________." It does not matter if you are correct about what is "true" for her. Rather, it is the process of considering the other person after having empathized with your own needs that fuels the shift. When you make this shift to compassion, you will have a greater potential to actually say what you want to say.

The other empathic choice is to give empathy to the other person out loud. Remember, it is not about being "right" with your guesses; it is about honoring the intention of connecting with the other. This intention reflects the spirit of satya, which is not just telling the truth but has inherent in it the desire to better the world. The best way to learn empathic guessing is to do it. Give yourself silent empathy all day long when judgments arise, and then try it with others. And watch the magic happen! (See the exercises at the end of the chapter for practice in offering empathic guessing.)

One important distinction to keep in mind when you are choosing empathy is the difference between empathy and sympathy. Empathy is focused on the other, on their feelings and needs. Sympathy is listening to the other and then shifting the emphasis to yourself as a way to connect—for example, "I know just how you feel; my dog died last March." While offering sympathy is often well-intentioned, it takes the focus of the communication from the other person and back to yourself. As a practice, notice when you use sympathy instead of using an empathetic guess.

One experience of giving empathy particularly stands out for me (Ike). In January 2002, in the aftermath of the attacks of September 11 and the kidnapping of *Wall Street Journal* reporter Daniel Pearl, NVC trainer John Kinyon and I offered three days of NVC conflict resolution training in the Shamsatu refugee camp, near Peshawar, Pakistan.

Our travels in Pakistan took us northwest, toward the Afghan border, near the Khyber Pass. We had to gain access to the camps from the head of security for all refugee camps for the 1.1 million Afghan refugees, Lt. Col. Abdula Hafeez. We answered his skeptical questions for nearly ten minutes as we tried to "sell" him on the idea of our offering a training, but he remained understandably reluctant to grant us permission. His shift from skepticism to willingness did not occur until we spent the next ten minutes guessing what he was feeling and needing. Then, in one of the fastest shifts I have ever seen, he leaned forward on his desk and wrote out a pass to the camp, complete with two security officers detailed to us, instructions to the camp administrator that he was to accompany us at all times, and a message to be sent ahead to the camp to invite all the elders to meet with us.

We offered the training session for the leaders of the various tribes represented in the camp, which held 1,100 families who had fled the many years of violence in Afghanistan. We had planned to teach the principles of NVC from day one, but there was so much pain being expressed that we could not move past giving empathy for the first two days. These people had lived in the so-called "temporary" camps for years; they had been promised so much by so many, and much of it had never materialized. They were no longer living in their country, their children did not have many of the things we take for granted, and their future was unsettled, to say the least.

Instead of spending our time teaching, as we had planned, we found ourselves responding to the immediate pain and anguish in front of us, which was directly stimulated by us being American. This anguish was created in part by what the United States had done in Afghanistan—by leaving as soon as the Soviets had withdrawn and not following through with promises of support. All the pain and suffering of nearly twenty-five years of turmoil and war boiled over in our interaction with these men.

With each cycle of empathy, we could see plainly the wonder of empathic connection. When our guesses about their feelings and needs turned out to be true for them, the speakers would fall silent, their eyes would lower, and the other twenty-five or so men sitting on the floor around the room would murmur together in assent. The muscles around the speaker's eyes would relax, his jaw would soften, and a glistening of tears would appear in his eyes. This would be followed by ten or twenty seconds of reflective silence without eye contact. We felt the empathic connection as a palpable entity. We went through tens of these cycles in the first two days alone.

We learned once again that needs are universal and are part of all human beings, even when those needs are translated from English to Urdu to Pastho and then at times into Uzbek, Tajik, Turkmen, or Parsi, via ad hoc translations. On the surface, our seeming differences of dress, life experiences, culture, education, and resources separated us, and yet, with the sharing of our feelings and needs, I saw beyond the differences to how we are all truly the same. These were men, just like me, who wanted to contribute to the well-being of their families and others, and who were distressed because they needed order and stability. They wanted education for their children. They wanted to trust that commitments when made would be kept. They were longing for hope, hope for a world where, as one man put it, doctors would work as doctors, and engineers as engineers, and shopkeepers as shopkeepers, referring to so many who were instead working at manual labor.

At the beginning of the last day, a Friday, the Islamic holy day, one of the men invited us to join him in prayer at the mosque that afternoon. Immediately another man objected, saying that we could not go to the mosque because we were not Muslim. We had been looking for a "real" conflict to use as an example in the group, and John Kinyon seized on this opportunity. I did have some concern that our role play was about something as real and sensitive as nonbelievers at Islamic prayer services, but we decided to go ahead, since this was actually what had arisen in the group.

The invitation to the mosque became our example of conflict. With some coaching, the needs were identified. Those who wanted us to join them in prayer at the mosque needed understanding, connection, and education. Those who objected needed respect for that which helped them make sense out of their world—their religion. Each side reflected back those needs to the other side. Then John asked his question: "Is there anyone here who does not share these needs?" An excited murmur of insight and awareness filled the room. Yes, of course, seemed to be the response, we see how we all share these needs, and we can respect them in ourselves and others.

The brainstorming for an actual strategy to meet the needs took only moments. In retrospect, our solution seemed simple, as they often do when each person feels heard. We all agreed that the Westerners in the room who had not been raised in Islam would receive a fifteen- or twenty-minute explanation of the ceremony, and that they would sit outside the doors of the mosque and observe from there. Finally, they would be welcomed into the mosque at the completion of Friday afternoon prayers. We had solved our "conflict" in a way that connected us to them, them to us, and all of us to each other. John and I were profoundly moved by the experience, one that still gives me hope for how the world can be.

At the end of the last session, one of the elders said to us, referring to the NVC training, "If we could do this, we would have no more war."

CHOICE 4: FOCUS ON OTHER: REQUEST

Once you have practiced self-expression and empathy for the other, it is time—and quickly—to make a request. There are two types of requests. The first is an *action request,* which is simply to ask for the action you would like the other person to take. While this sounds easy, we have often found it to be difficult.

After 9/11, Ike and I (Judith) wanted to write a letter to the president expressing our feelings and needs and making requests about the course we wanted him to take. We found that we could very easily write what we didn't want him to do, but it took several days for us to come up with and write what we did want him to do. We wrote that we wanted him to respond using a model of justice and police enforcement rather than a military model.

While Ike was applying NVC in legal mediations, I attempted to apply NVC as I taught my yoga classes. I liked how using NVC helped me make clear requests of my students. In a way, every time I say to my yoga class "Utthita Trikonasana," I am making a request. But I cannot "make" the student do the pose; I can really only ask. So the question is, how will I ask? Will I ask in a way that will be more likely to have my request granted? Or will I ask in a way that is perceived as a demand? When I make a demand, I create a distance between the student and me. If instead I make a true request, I am remaining open not only in my choice of words but also to how they are received. When I make a request instead of a demand, I speak from a deep respect for the student and for myself. I predict that requesting with awareness, respect, and openness will create connection between the student and me. This is what I want: connection and compassion between human beings. I can begin to create this connection when I am clear about whether I am demanding or requesting.

Whether I am making a request or a demand is not determined by the way my sentence sounds. Instead, I know the difference by how I feel inside my body if the request or demand is refused. If it was a request, I will just ask again in another way and attempt to find out what might be keeping the student from meeting my request. If my request was really a demand, then I will react in my body, often with feelings that come from thinking that the student should do what I am asking.

As a yoga teacher, before I studied NVC, I occasionally felt irritated when a student in class did not respond to my demand, but I never understood why I felt that way. I may ask a student to attempt Urdhva Mukha Vrksasana (Handstand), and she may be hesitant. Am I demanding or requesting? How can I request in a way that will make it delicious for the student to choose Handstand?

If I make a true action request, then this delicious choice is a real possibility. With my intention, I have opened the world by reminding myself and the student to hold as precious the understanding that we are all at choice. This is a deeply rewarding way to communicate, in part because it so accurately reflects the way the world actually is. By asking, "Are you willing to . . . ," I make it clear that I only want people to do what they are willing to do. On the one hand, if they act on my request from a place of obligation, even if they do what I want, we will both "pay," and it won't be satisfying for either of us. On the other hand, if the other person responds to my request with willingness, we are connecting to meet each other's needs. The fulfilling of the request becomes almost a form of service in the spiritual sense of the word. The second type of request is a *process request*. This type of request is asking the other person one of two questions: Would you tell me what you just heard me say? Or, how do you feel hearing what I just said?

We have found both of these requests to be very useful. The first, "Would you tell me what you just heard me say," is an attempt to make sure that the message you sent with your observations, feelings, and needs was the message that was actually received. This process can sometimes be like the children's game Whisper, where each child in a circle of children whispers a phrase to the next, and so on to the last child, who says it out loud. The game is funny because the phrase reported by the last person is never even close to what the first child whispered.

It happens with adult communication, too. You may think that you're being very clear, but what the other person hears may be somehow not what you said or intended. Check this out with a friend or with your empathy buddy. Try reflecting what you hear or asking for what you said until the sender of the message is satisfied that they have been heard correctly.

By asking the person to tell you what they heard, you are meeting your needs for clarity and connection. It is important that the other person understands that this is not a test of their abilities. You can make that clear by listening to what they say and responding with some form of "thank you," such as, "Thank you for your willingness to tell me what you heard." We suggest that you thank them, regardless of what the other person says back to you. They have done what you asked, which was to tell you what they heard. If they heard something different from what you wanted to say, now you know that, and you can try again to be heard as you would like. If you are satisfied that they understood what you were saying, then proceed with the communication by making the request again or by making another request.

If you are not satisfied that the person got what you said, then try again. Break down your communication into smaller bites. One way to do this might be to say, "I would like you to hear something different, so let me say it this way." Give them a smaller piece of what is true for you, using fewer words, if possible. Then ask them again to tell you what they heard. If they react negatively to this, start over with self-empathy and empathy for the other. Maybe they are not able to reflect back what you said because they are still in need of empathy. When you are satisfied that you have been heard, you may want to proceed further.

The second process request, "How do you feel hearing what I just said," is an attempt, in a shorthand way, to assess whether the listener's needs are being met or not. You may have just said something that has a great deal of meaning for the other. She may be overwhelmed or confused by what you just said. The communication most likely will not proceed as you want if the other person feels irritated, for instance, by what you are saying, and you don't realize it. Also, by asking the other to tell you what is alive in her, what she is feeling, you are helping her to connect with her own inner states. You are stimulating self-awareness in the other. And you are using your words to connect you both to the present moment. This is the essence of spiritual speech.

PRACTICING NONVIOLENT COMMUNICATION

Practicing self-empathy

- Find a quiet place, and remember an interaction of the past week that you did not enjoy. Now write down a self-empathy phrase about it. Begin with the observation, then write your feelings, and guess your needs that were not met by what was said or done. If you have difficulty guessing what you were feeling or needing, set the paper aside and revisit it tomorrow or the next day. Keep at it until you feel the internal shift we get from receiving empathy, even from ourselves.
- The next time someone stimulates a reaction in you, say, "Excuse me for five minutes." Then go into another room, and give yourself empathy until you feel curious about what is going on with the other person. Then return to conversation. (If you do not feel curious, that

is a sign you need more self-empathy. Continue giving yourself empathy about your feelings and needs until you begin to care about the other person in the situation.)

Practicing self-expression

- Tell someone close to you, perhaps your empathy buddy, that you are experimenting with a new way of communicating. Then ask them to listen as you say something with your old style of communicating and then with your newly learned NVC way of expressing. Remember the sentence, "When I hear you say that, I feel ___________, because my need for ___________ is not met. Would you be willing to ___________?" Try this process at least once each day until it becomes more familiar and less awkward.
- Use self-expression when you call a technical help line or customer service number. Follow the "training wheels" sentence in chapter 2, and listen to how effective it is in this context. I (Judith) used my calls to customer service lines when I was learning NVC to practice. The first time I did it, I felt a little silly, but not only did I get excellent service, the representative called me back in ten minutes with a solution to my problem that moments before she said would take a week. Begin with empathy for the other. One way to

COMMUNICATION CHOICES

Where Is My Focus?	*Silent Communication*	*Spoken Communication*
On myself	Choice 1. Self-Empathy: Naming to myself what I am observing, feeling, needing, requesting	Choice 2. Self-Expression: Saying how I am feeling and requesting what I would like without blame, criticism, or demand
On the other person	Choice 3. Silent Empathy: Guessing what the other is observing, feeling, needing, requesting	Choice 3. Giving Empathy: Guessing how another is feeling and what they might be requesting without blame, criticism, or demand
On the other person		Choice 4. Making a Request: Making an action request or a process request, asking for feedback

THE TWO TYPES OF REQUESTS

Action requests:	A strategy to meet everyone's needs: "Would you be willing to . . . ?"
Process requests:	For reflection: "Would you tell me what you heard me say?" For response: "How do you feel hearing what I say?"

start is: "Hello, I can imagine that you are really busy today, but I really want you to hear how important this is to me."

Giving empathy

- The next time you are waiting in line at the airport or in a store and your turn comes up, open the conversation by giving empathy to the person behind the counter. Say something like, "Are you feeling overwhelmed by the number of customers?" or "It looks like you are really busy today and have lots of unhappy customers." Notice how the person responds.
- Today, when someone complains to you about the government, the weather, or his favorite sports team, instead of joining in, respond with empathy. Say something like, "So when you say that, are you wanting me to hear how irritated you are by what ________ (name the person) did about that issue?" Continue to give empathy until the person begins to shift and a feeling of connection occurs. It may take several rounds of empathy. Or it may take several conversations until they feel heard. You might use something like this as well: "It sounds like her actions did not meet your needs for integrity and compassion." Observe how the other person begins to change and how much more connected you feel.

Making a request

- Whenever you want something from someone today, say, "Are you willing to . . ." when you ask for it. Be sure to be specific about what you are asking her to do. For example, "Are you willing to make your bed and hang up your clothes by 6 p.m., when our guests are arriving?"
- The next time you are in a meeting, observe how people do not make clear requests of others. They often say things like, "Yes, let's do that" or "That sounds like a great idea," but they do not request a specific action from specific people at a specific time.

4

LISTENING TO OURSELVES AND OTHERS

Human beings are perhaps never more frightening than when they are convinced beyond doubt that they are right.

—LAURENS VAN DER POST

IN ONE OF my early seminars with Marshall Rosenberg, he said something that stimulated anger in me (Judith). His words were: "Never do anything that doesn't give you the joy of a three-year-old feeding a hungry duck." While I liked the vividness of this image, my response was swift and emotional. I said to myself, "Well then, I wouldn't do half my life. We have to do things we don't want to do, or life would fall apart."

Immediately I began to observe my reaction to his words and to give myself empathy for the words that had bubbled up in response to his. But for several years I found that I could not accept what he had said. I had beliefs or judgments about it, like, "Doing only what you want to do is indulgent and selfish." I did not enjoy the language I was using toward myself; I did not enjoy the judgments I was having about myself for having those judgments. I was caught in a hall of mirrors; I was judging myself for judging myself.

This circle of judgment is a common process for many people. The way we listen to our self-dialogue can be one of compassion or one of judgment, but whichever we choose, it is a powerfully life-shaping process. My (internal) words reflect my thoughts, and my thoughts reflect my beliefs, and these beliefs, especially the unconscious ones, run my life. The practice of *satya* and right speech begins at home, when I give myself empathy for my beliefs. These days my inner dialogue is shaped by NVC. It clearly hasn't always been so.

When I was growing up, I "heard" many messages from my family, culture, and church that told me to deny my needs. I am not saying those were the lessons that were taught, but they were the lessons I heard. I was taught that to do so was right and unselfish and in service to God. So I learned to get my needs met by the strategy of not really asking for what I needed. In fact, I tried specifically to not reveal what I needed, in order to avoid being judged as "needy" or demanding. I do not believe I am alone in this; women especially seem to be raised as I was: trained to look after everyone else's needs and to deny the existence of their own. "I live to serve" was my motto. Marshall Rosenberg addresses this issue when he states provocatively but kindly, "Women have no needs." Of course, he is trying to draw our attention to this issue by making such a ridiculous statement. Unfortunately, the statement was all too true for me. Or so it seemed.

Remember, to acknowledge our needs is not to be demanding. All human needs are the expression of life's energy flowing through us. Needs are the very thing that connect us to life itself. When we become aware of our needs and the needs of others and long to meet those needs, we are honoring the sacredness of life.

As I have learned, the problem with living in a way that denies my needs is that it sets the stage for me to do violence to myself. That violence is taken out on me by me, but it could just as well be taken out on another. If I act from violence to myself or others, I am not contributing to the peaceful world I want to create. I am not living from my highest values. I am not living the spirit of satya or right speech.

If I do something for you because I should, or because it is "spiritual" to act that way, or because it makes me a "good person," a residue will be left. This residue is often resentment, and resentment poisons relationships and diminishes life. Paradoxically, I will end up taking it out on you, because in a twisted way I blame you for me not getting my needs met.

In order to learn more about my own needs, I began to check in with myself several times a day to see what I happened to be needing at that moment. I would then give myself empathy. And I found out something interesting. I always could guess what I was feeling, but I had a hard time guessing what I was needing. Ike, on the other hand, always knew what he was needing but did not seem to know what he was feeling. He later reported that at that period of his life he had only two feelings: OK and angry.

I began to observe that I frequently did things not because they met my needs but because I was afraid of the judgment that I predicted would come from the other person if I said no. For example, Ike would ask me to go to the movies, and even if I didn't want to go, I would say yes. Then, when we went to the movie, I would complain about it and somehow make it hard for us to enjoy ourselves. Or I would say no to going to the movie, then feel guilty about saying no, and be "too nice" to him for the next couple of days. I bounced between resentment and being overly nice; I thought that was what a marriage relationship was.

THE DUCK INDEX

Because of my personal lack of awareness about my needs, I realized I needed a specific strategy to help me learn and practice. So I created what I call the "duck index." I love the image of a squealing, delighted little child running and throwing pieces of stale bread for a flock of ducks by a lake. I smile every time I think of it.

My duck index has a scale of 1 to 10. I decided I would not do anything unless it was at least a 6 on my index, and then I would see what happened. As I used the duck index, I learned first to get in touch with my needs and then to trust that understanding. The next time Ike asked me to a movie I didn't want to see, I checked in with myself and responded with, "That's a 3 on my duck index." But that was not the end of the matter. The next thing I said was, "But seduce me with your needs."

In other words, just because someone asks us to do something we don't want to do, something that is not high on our duck index, doesn't mean the negotiation is closed. We could be open to shifting. Shifting is not at all the same as giving in. Just saying yes to all requests is giving in. To shift is to hear the needs of the other and to feel that to meet them would also meet your needs.

So when I said, "Seduce me with your needs," I was acknowledging this reality. I was telling Ike that I was open to shifting so that meeting his needs would also meet mine. Marshall Rosenberg states, "My needs first and foremost, but never my needs at the expense of your needs." Shifting is the process of attempting to meet both my needs and the needs of the other person.

Remember two things about the distinction between strategies and needs. Strategies are ways of getting needs met, and needs are never in conflict; only strategies are in conflict. At any given time, there are always many strategies that can meet any particular need. When we cling to a specific strategy as the only way to meet a need, we suffer if that strategy does not bear fruit.

In the preceding example, the movie was not a need; it was a strategy for getting a need met. When I asked Ike what needs he was attempting to meet by suggesting we go to the movie, he said his needs were fun, entertainment, and companionship. When I heard those needs, I immediately shifted from a 3 to a 5 on my duck index. I felt an actual shift in my body. After a couple more rounds of sharing needs and empathy, I was still at a 5 and so did not "force" myself to go. Then we brainstormed about other ways we might both get our needs met, and we ended up satisfied. The whole thing took ten minutes, and we ended the evening still in connection with each other.

So what happens when I agree to do something because it is an 8 on my duck index, but when the time comes to follow through, it might have gone down to a 4? This happens to all of us occasionally. On Monday the idea of going to my friend's party on Friday night is an 8, but after a long week, when Friday night arrives, and it's raining, and I'm tired, going to the party seems like a 4. How do I meet my need for rest and my friend's need for companionship at the same time?

First and always, give yourself empathy for the lack of enthusiasm you are feeling right now about following through with the plan. In other words, guess specifically what is alive in you now. When that process feels complete, and you are connected fully with your needs, then connect now with the needs you were trying to meet then, when you said yes. Again give yourself empathy. When that is complete, give silent empathy to your friend. What needs is she attempting to meet by inviting you to the party?

The last step is to call your friend and express your needs. Tell her what is true for you. It might go something like this: "On Monday, when I said I would come to the party, I was excited. But now I have a great need for rest. How do you feel hearing that?" When she tells you her feelings, give her empathy for whatever you guess is up for her—perhaps hurt or disappointment. Once you have made empathic connection with her, ask, "Would you be willing to brainstorm for five minutes other strategies we can use to meet both your need for companionship (assuming that is the need) and my need for rest?"

Here is a crucial point: be open to any outcome. A number of things could happen. She could be totally fine with you not coming, or you could shift and decide to go after talking to her and extrapolating her needs, or you could both decide to get together tomorrow, or you could agree that you would take a nap and come to the party later. The point is that, through this process, you would both get your needs met.

It may sound like all this would take some time, and it does. But how much time would it take to not go through this process of connection? How much time and suffering would disconnection with your needs and your friend's needs cost in the long run?

Many people are reluctant to ask for their needs to be met because they believe their needs are a burden to others. This way of thinking has two consequences. First, you don't allow others the gift of giving you what you need. Think of a baby. Babies do not hesitate to ask for their needs to be met, and they tend to do so strongly and immediately. But as adults, we often hide our needs, because we feel they are not worthy of being met. Even if my needs are not a gift to you, I like how I behave when I choose to think they are.

It might be useful here to remember the distinction between requesting and demanding. Making a demand for your needs to be met, or a demand for anything, is to not include the other in the process. Demanding implies that there are consequences, presumably negative consequences, for the other person if they do not do as you ask. Requesting means you are open to the outcome. One more suggestion: When you are beginning to use the duck index, we suggest that you use it for simple, everyday decisions. The duck index may not work well for you at first if you start using it with life's major challenges.

PLEASE AND THANK YOU

Another way to listen in a new way to your inner voice is to hear whatever anyone says to you as a request. Specifically, translate everything anyone says to you as either a "please" or a "thank you." This is one of my (Judith's) favorite techniques.

Here's how to do it. One day I stopped my car at a red light and was a little bit too far into the crosswalk. A man who was crossing yelled at me, calling me a stupid driver. I would usually take this sort of thing to heart and feel terrible about my actions. My inner dialogue would be filled with lots of judgments about myself. Other people might do the opposite, thinking how stupid or rude the man was being.

On that day, I decided to try hearing what he said as a request, in particular as a "please," a technique I had just learned. So I said to myself, What if he said it this way: "Please hear how afraid I was that you might have hit me and injured me." When I translated "stupid driver" into "please hear my fear," I felt compassion arise in me for him and for myself. I really liked how I felt about the situation then; I was just a human being, as was he, doing the best we could. I felt neither angry at him nor angry at myself. It was a red-letter day.

Another example is a conversation I had with my teenage daughter. She asked me to pick her up after school, adding, "And Mom, please don't act like a dork." I could have chosen to respond with hurt or by correcting her for being "rude," but instead I chose to hear the following: "Mom, please hear how tender I am around my friends. I am so afraid they will reject me, and I don't want to give them any ammunition to do that. Please help me by not standing out and attracting any attention." Whether or not this statement was what she was feeling and needing, I liked how I shifted to a more compassionate state when I decided to hear it that way. William James said, "The greatest weapon we have to combat stress is the ability to choose our thoughts." When we choose to hear the other's statement as "please hear my pain," we have the choice to act in a way that will connect us with them. This ability to choose to react to those around us with awareness is what makes speech a spiritual practice.

"Thank you" is another thing people say to us all day long. When they say, "That was a great yoga class" or "I really enjoyed the meal; it was good," they are saying "thank you." When I hear that I was good or did something good, I feel vaguely uneasy. I know that if I am good, I can also be bad. Once I am on the good–bad or right–wrong continuum, I can go either way. I may not be able to do it again or in the right way, and I feel nervous about that.

But now, instead of hearing their statement as being about me, I hear it as being about them. I translate what they are saying into a request: "Please hear how much your class (or meal) met my needs." When I translate their statements into "thank you for meeting my needs," I am reinforcing the understanding that I am not the source of another's happiness. The fact that I met their needs was about their needs getting met, not about me being good or right. Hearing their statement as a request for me to understand that needs were met makes it simpler and cleaner. I am only part of the dance of communication then, and I like being partners with others in that way.

PRACTICING NONVIOLENT COMMUNICATION

Duck index

- Tell your family or roommates about the duck index, and begin to practice it over small things, like what you would like for dinner or what time you want to go shopping with them. Celebrate your newfound clarity.
- The next time someone asks a favor of you that is low on your duck index, say, "That's not high on my duck

index, but seduce me with your needs." Be open to shifting, so that it might become something you want to do. Only say yes if you have shifted.

Please and thank you

- Notice today how often someone says "thank you" to you. After one of those times, ask the person to tell you exactly what you said or did that caused them to say "thank you."
- Think of a time in the last couple of days when you said something in irritation to someone close to you, such as, "Why are you always late?" Translate your statement of irritation into a "please" statement. If possible, go back to the other person and say, "What I really meant to say the other day was 'Please hear how afraid I felt when you did not come home at the time we agreed and did not call me to say you were OK.' I was upset because I care about you and your well-being, and I wanted you to know that." Note their response.

5

WHAT WE SAY MATTERS

People heal by having an authentic connection with an authentic human being.

—MARTIN BUBER

MANY YEARS AGO, I (Judith) had a conversation with Usharbudh Arya (now Swami Veda), a practitioner of yoga since childhood and a scholar of Sanskrit and the ancient texts of India. My question was, "Which is more important, the practice of *ahimsa,* nonharming, or the practice of *satya,* truth?" (Both are part of *yama,* or the first limb of the traditional yoga of Patanjali.) I wanted to know how to choose between these yamas in my practice. Should I tell someone the truth that might hurt them, or tell them something "kind" instead, to avoid harming them?

Swamiji's answer surprised me. He said, "Something cannot be true and unkind at the same time." This answer still echoes in my ears as I attempt to use the techniques of Nonviolent Communication to express my desire to practice satya and right speech. Both Ike and I have talked about the seeming conflict between truth and nonharming, and we have clarified for ourselves two values for guiding our speech that we feel reflect Swami Veda's wisdom.

First, we hold that speech is a *power* that we can choose to use for fostering connection between and among people. In order to do that, however, we must first connect with ourselves. This ability to turn inward and be in connection with self in a truthful way lies at the heart of spiritual speech. Without self awareness, it is likely that you will not speak with the words you want.

Second, we believe that "truth" is what is alive in me at this very moment. That is my truth. I can only speak from what is alive in me right now. Not only is this all I can do, but it is the best way to bring my connection with others to life. When I speak from what is alive in me right now, I am present with myself. When I speak from that space, I model and encourage others to do the same.

This practice will change the world. It will change your life, and it will affect others in a profound and distinct way. When you create an atmosphere of trust and connection with your words, there is little that cannot get worked out between people. What greater gift can we give the world than our own true selves?

I once heard Marshall Rosenberg state in a seminar what it means to speak in a "spiritual" way: "It respects the conditions in which all members of the world community can live in dignity and freedom, without destroying each other's chances of livelihood, society, or culture." This is a practical expression of spiritual speech, and it expresses values that Ike and I both hold dear. *What we say matters*, not only because it changes the immediate relationship we are in right now, but also because it shapes the future by leaving a legacy of clarity and connection among human beings.

DEALING WITH ANGER

The experience of anger and its expression in speech is a daily experience for most of us. One day I decided to count the number of times I felt frustration, irritation, or anger. I bought a small handheld counter and counted every little ripple that arose. The number at the end of the day was astounding to me: sixty-seven.

Perhaps that is not a typical number, but with road rage and violence all around us, perhaps it is. As Marshall Rosenberg points out, and as we have experienced in our own lives, anger, shame, guilt, and depression are a special class of feelings that arise out of judging how the world should be.

With feelings like joy, connection, or disappointment, there is nothing hidden underneath the feeling. But if you inquire further of yourself, you will find other feelings lurking underneath anger. These hidden feelings are usually one or a combination of hurt, fear, or frustration.

This was hard for us to hear. Ike reports that in the beginning of his study of NVC, the only two feelings he could really identify were OK and angry. I (Judith) remember the first time I learned from a meditation teacher about the arising of anger. The practice she was giving was to be present with what was arising within us as we sat on the cushion. That was it, no other technique. Furthermore, she suggested that beginning meditation students typically spend most of the first few years on the meditation cushion realizing how angry they are.

Believe it or not, this profound teaching stimulated irritation in me. (How ironic.) Then I began a consistent meditation practice and realized how right she was. What I usually felt was not a full-blown fury but rather the "little anger" of mild frustration, of irritation, of wishing it were different, whatever "it" was—wishing my back didn't hurt, wishing the neighbor would stop mowing her lawn at 6:30 a.m. when I was trying to meditate, wishing I was not feeling irritated at the neighbor. This mental process of irritation (or even anger) can continue and echo through the mind almost forever, or so it would seem.

Take a quiet moment and remember a time recently when you felt angry. Reflect now on how you felt then. As you consider it, give yourself empathy by guessing now what was alive in you in that moment of anger. It's very likely you will discover that at its root it was hurt, frustration, or fear. One of these three emotions is probably a more accurate expression of what you were feeling underneath your anger at the time.

When you discover what was alive in you, you will shift. This shift, as mentioned before, will be not only a shift in perception but also a shift in bodily sensation. For me this shift is a verification that I have discovered my truth.

One day I decided to test this theory. The next time I remembered something that day that had stimulated anger in me, I connected with myself using the process of self-empathy. I noticed immediately that I was in my head, telling myself over and over, "How could he say that to me? Who does he think he is?"

Then I purposely focused on the sensations in my belly and tried to guess what feeling might really be alive in me. Suddenly I got it; I wasn't angry really; I was hurt when I recalled what the other person had said. When I began to think again about what the other had said, I immediately moved into my thoughts, and I felt anger again. Down to the belly and into feeling, up to the head and lost in thoughts and judgment: I did this dance four or five times, a smile slowly growing across my face. I finally understood. Anger was stimulated by my thoughts and judgments about the situation and was a strategy for hiding my feeling of hurt. My anger was helping me protect myself from hurt. I was building a wall of protection, using anger as my tool.

One day Ike and I entered a large hall for a seminar. I noticed a man across the room who I labeled "the angry man." When the moderator asked us to take a seat away from the person we had come with, I made a beeline to a seat as far as I could get from the man I had labeled. Of course, he came and sat by me, and we ended up being partners for a number of exercises. Ironically, if we are living our own anger, we tend to attract it in others. Not only that, but if we have unresolved anger, we tend to scan the environment looking for it in others. We will always find it, just as I did in the seminar.

When was the last time your anger reached another person's heart? Anger is not effective in connecting us with ourselves or with others. It is not an effective tool for communicating with those we care about.

The next time you find yourself angry with someone, take some time to give yourself empathy until you recognize what you are telling yourself that is causing you to feel angry. Then empathize with the need you are seeking to meet by what you're saying to yourself. Chances are you will be much happier with what you say to the other person if you take care of yourself first.

RIGHTEOUS ANGER AND SOCIAL CHANGE

Most of us are familiar with the term "righteous anger." It is used to mean the anger that has a "good" or socially acceptable cause. Actually, our anger can have a righteous quality. We are often angry when we believe we are right. You would never say, "I am so mad at you, and I am completely wrong." Feeling that you are right always fuels anger. And anger disconnects us from ourselves and from others. Please note, though, that we are not talking about the anger we all feel about child abuse or racism; instead, this is the kind of anger we feel when we believe our ego has been attacked.

A Buddhist story addresses the issue of righteous anger. One day a monk found an abandoned rowboat by the shore of the lake near his monastery. After trying unsuccessfully to find the owner of the rowboat, he spent his free time restoring it. The day finally came to launch the beautiful new boat. It was a little misty on the lake, but he settled into the boat and rowed out onto the water. Suddenly out of the mist came another rowboat, and it plowed into his new boat and damaged its prow. The monk got angry and thought, "Who would be so careless as to run into me and damage my boat?" I am guessing that this anger was fueled by the thought that he was right and had been wronged by the person in the other boat.

As the other boat came closer, it turned out to be empty; it had just drifted into his boat. With that, the monk's anger melted away. There was no one to blame. When we can recognize this righteous, ego-based anger for what it is, we understand our needs and the needs of others, and we are more likely to choose words that reflect that understanding. *Everything is an empty rowboat.*

While we may feel a strong commitment to social change, fueling it with ego-based anger disconnects us from the heart of compassion. Acting from ego-based anger can prevent us from practicing ahimsa in its deepest form. When you want to change some circumstance, first use self-empathy to connect yourself to your needs, and then act in a way that furthers the social change you value.

ENEMY IMAGES

One of the surest ways to disconnect from ourselves and temporarily forget the values of satya and right speech is to project enemy images onto other people or even onto ourselves. This projection can be onto our family, neighbors, or political figures we have never met. When we have enemy images, we make a moralistic judgment about ourselves or others, believing that they or we are evil.

When you are in conflict with someone and you tell yourself negative judgments about them, these enemy images leak out and color the interaction. Whatever I think of you will influence my body language, my expression, and my words. And you will sense these judgments, even if I don't express them with words. Connection will be difficult, if not impossible.

Carrying enemy images into a meeting or conversation almost guarantees that you will not get your needs met. If you are going into a meeting or conversation with someone for whom you have enemy images, do self-empathy and then silent empathy for the other until your feelings have shifted. This may take days or even weeks.

You may also choose to seek the help of an experienced NVC trainer to help you with this issue, if you are in a lot of pain. You may even want to write out your goals—of ahimsa and connection, for example—on a piece of paper and have that in front of you while you talk with the other person. It will help you to stay focused on your values throughout the meeting.

Make no mistake: Acknowledging our enemy images, choosing to transform them by finding the need behind the judgment, and getting help to do this is not work for the fainthearted. Society supports the habits of thinking and talking using enemy images. But if we are committed to self-transformation and the transformation of the world, we will learn to speak from a place without enemy images.

Let's be clear: Transforming enemy images does not mean we give up passion for our values or belief in our cause. It does mean that we do not put the other person or ourselves in a box labeled "evil, wrong, or bad" and then try to interact with them. We can certainly disagree with others' actions and choices, even to the point of believing that they should be incarcerated to protect those around them. But the practice of nonharming is to see the other person as a human being who is suffering, as we all are, and to think, act, and speak from compassion. NVC is a powerful tool for helping us to do exactly that.

THE JOY OF INTERRUPTING

Marshall Rosenberg reports that, in some countries in the world, no one will interrupt you, even in an unproductive conversation, but will wait until you are finished before they speak. In other countries, however, people tend to talk all at once in gatherings and meetings. The advantage of this, he jokes, is that they can have the same unproductive conversation in half the time!

I now believe that no one ever interrupts me. That is not to say that people do not occasionally speak when I am speaking. But I choose not to hear this as interruption. Instead, I choose to hear their enthusiasm about sharing something with me. I believe that perception does not shape your life; it *is* your life.

If I tell myself that you are interrupting me, I might feel irritated because my need for respect is not being met. If I understand your "interrupting" as your eagerness to give me your insight or idea, I would feel quite different. Either way, I am creating my own environment. Minute by minute, we all shape our internal environment, and from that comes the happiness or suffering of our lives. Using the tools of self-empathy and then empathy for the other allows us to hear their words not as rudeness but as an exchange we can enjoy.

But what about interrupting someone else? Is there ever a time to do that? When I was growing up, interrupting anyone at any time was strictly prohibited. So when I first heard Marshall Rosenberg speak about the importance of sometimes interrupting someone else, I was shocked. I wondered how interrupting could ever be nonviolent.

But I have shifted on this issue. Here's why. First, if I listen to you past the time I am interested or truly able to hear, I am actually disconnecting from you and doing violence to myself. Before in my life when I felt disconnected from a conversation, I pretended to listen to be polite, but I'm now sure that my eyes glazed over and the other person knew I was tuning out. Other people know when we are not present. They often respond by moving closer, speaking louder, or repeating the story. Is it really practicing ahimsa to pretend to listen when we aren't?

I have since learned to respond in another way. When I feel myself drifting away from what another is saying to me, first I tune in to myself to see what is alive in me; this involves silent self-empathy. Then I might say something like, "I'm hearing that you're excited to tell me about this, but right now there are more words than I can take in because I'm tired (assuming it is true that I am feeling tired). Can we pick another time to have this conversation when I'm predicting I'll be more able to listen?"

Another way is to first acknowledge what is going on for you at that moment. It might sound like this: "I hear that you really want to share this story with me, but I'm not able to listen fully because I'm feeling pressed for time. My husband is by the door, waiting for me to leave for an appointment, and I'm anxious about being late for it. Can we set up a time tomorrow to talk on the phone so you can finish your story? I'd love to hear it then."

Try this truth telling, and you will be amazed at how people will understand and support your predicament. Often others will be relieved by your words, because they were feeling uneasy, as they felt your attention and energy pulling away. I like this approach because it beautifully combines ahimsa, satya, and right speech. It is speech as spiritual practice.

In the long run, it is actually more loving and compassionate to speak your satya—what is alive in you—and to connect with the other person by "interrupting" than to stay silent, seemingly listening but really drifting away from them. That is not what they want, I am guessing, nor is it what you want. Speak your truth in a way designed to promote connection, and you reduce the violence you do to them, to the relationship, and of course to yourself.

REPEATING THE STORY

Have you ever stood and listened as a friend, coworker, or acquaintance told you the same story over and over, until you wanted to run away? Usually what happens is that they tell you about a painful incident from their past, and when your response does not meet their need for empathy, they tell it again, sometimes in a louder voice, or sometimes the next time you see them. This may be because we have been educated to think that the most important thing in the world is what other people think about us.

As speakers, we may have done this as well. We are confusing understanding and empathy. Usually we think that what we want most is to be understood by the other person, but what we probably actually want is empathy. Because we think we want to be understood, and through that understanding to experience a kind of healing, we tell the story over and over. Ironically, this strategy not only fails to satisfy our need to be understood, but it can also alienate us from the listener.

To practice spiritual speech is to hear not what someone thinks, but to hear the feelings and needs behind the words. When someone tells you what they are thinking about an experience or event, it will probably not connect them with their pain in a way that is healing. When someone tells you a story over and over, offer them your empathy by guessing what is going on with them. It might sound something like this: "When you say that, are you wanting me to get how much pain that caused you then, how much pain you are still in about it, and how much you may have been longing for respect (or clarity, or whatever it was)?"

When you offer an empathic guess as to what is going on for them at this moment, it is much more likely that they will shift into the present moment and into a connection with you. When you lead them gently into an empathic connection, you both will probably enjoy the moment more. When you do this, typically the person will stop telling the story, and you will stop pulling away.

When we speak our truth, we share what is real inside us. Then not only are we living in the present, we are also building a bridge to our authentic selves and to the authentic selves of others.

PRACTICING NONVIOLENT COMMUNICATION

Anger

- Remember the last time you were angry about a small thing. Sit quietly and give yourself silent empathy about the incident, guessing with compassion what really might have been alive in you. Note how your feelings shift.
- Spend a day noticing what it takes to stimulate anger in you. Whatever those things are, you are giving them tremendous power in your life. Use self-empathy when those thoughts arise.

Enemy images

- Think about someone you don't know but have enemy images about—for example, a public figure. Imagine a conversation with that person in which you give them empathy. Notice how you shift.
- The next time you have a meeting with a person or group about an issue, notice who in the room stimulates your enemy images. During the meeting, give them silent empathy.

Telling a story over and over

- The next time someone repeats a story to you, notice how you pull away and how they respond to that pulling away.
- What stories do you repeat to others? What might be the unmet need that drives the retelling? When you can, give yourself empathy around it.

6

TALKING TO OUR PARTNERS

Speak when you are angry—and you will make
the best speech you'll ever regret.

—LAURENCE J. PETER

FEW THINGS TEST our ability to be present and to grow as human beings as much as our most intimate relationships. Those relationships can stimulate our deepest emotions, both those we enjoy and those we don't, and can stimulate our strongly held patterns of speaking and acting. It is certainly never dull being in such a relationship. Ike and I think there should be a kind of yoga called "relationship yoga." It certainly is as challenging to relate to our partners with consistency and love over many years as it is to practice any yoga pose!

One day Ike and I were driving on a trip. I asked him what I thought was a simple question: "Are you thirsty?"

He responded to the exact question asked and said, "No." My response to him was irritation. When I tell this story in workshops, people often laugh. I believe they recognize themselves as either the questioner or the respondent.

Because of my upbringing and my beliefs, I asked Ike if he was thirsty as a way of saying that *I was thirsty*. As strange as that might sound to some readers, that was my typical pattern of asking for what I wanted. I was really trying to say, "I'm thirsty. Would you be willing to stop for some water?" But I had learned to never ask, or certainly to never ask directly, for my needs to be met. I believed that to ask for what I wanted was selfish, demanding, and not spiritual. My strategy was to use language to protect myself from what I imagined would be the other person's judgments about my needs. I disguised my needs by speaking in a way that made the need seem to be about them, not about me. Clearly, this way of operating had ramifications for all the interactions that Ike and I had.

As we learned Nonviolent Communication, things gradually changed. First, I shifted in my beliefs about my needs, and then I shifted my speech. Now I would say, "I'm thirsty. Would you be willing to stop for some water? Anyone else want water?" In this way of speaking, I am being as clear as I can about what is alive in me. Therefore I believe I am practicing *satya* and right speech as well.

Our culture fosters an assumption that many women absorb: *Women are not to have any needs.* Many men seem to absorb the teaching from the culture that *men are not to have any feelings*. Of course these rigid notions are a strategy to help people feel safe. But the irony is that we feel much safer in relationships when we are clear about our feelings and needs. This is true for two basic reasons.

First, we feel safer when our partner reveals what he is feeling, because unexpressed feelings are often received as aggression. We sense when someone is angry or upset, especially if we live with that person in an intimate relationship. So when they express their feelings in a way that we can hear, we often feel relief, even if we don't have a solution to the stimulus for their feelings.

One day our family visited another family just as that marriage was beginning to unravel. As I was unpacking my suitcase, our three children came into the bedroom, closed the door, and asked what was going on in that family, one they had known all their lives. I told them simply that what they were feeling was very likely the feeling that often prevails in homes where the partners are on the verge of separating. I was surprised at how much relief our children expressed. They felt the disturbed energy all around them and thus were reassured when someone they trusted validated their feelings.

Men are often taught to hide their vulnerability. They may have experienced shame or embarrassment in the past when they expressed their feelings, so they feel safer when they don't. In order to support your partner, especially if he is a man, you might say something like this: "I don't feel as connected to you as I like to be when you don't reveal your feelings to me" or "I feel so much safer with you when you tell me what you're feeling." We suggest that you immediately follow statements like these with a request, such as, "How do you feel hearing what I just said?"

How you respond to what your partner says next will strongly influence their willingness to reveal themselves to you in the future. We suggest that you respond with genuine appreciation for their willingness to answer, regardless of whether you like the content of the message. Your appreciation can be genuine, even if the content of the message stimulates pain in you, if you focus on the gift the person has given by revealing himself. We encourage you not to respond with a judgment about those feelings or reject them as incorrect or wrong. We can teach our partners to act in a way that they have labeled as "vulnerable" all their lives by the way we respond to any first steps they take to share their feelings with us.

Sometimes people, especially men, are taught to believe that feelings get in the way of "getting things done," so they must deny their feelings to be productive and thus worthy. But we can help our partners to realize that in the safe circle of the relationship, vulnerability and the sharing of feelings will not only be received with love, it will be celebrated.

The second thing to keep in mind about feelings and needs in intimate relationships is this: Women may have been educated not only to not ask for their needs to be met, but often they aren't even aware of what their needs are. Sigmund Freud famously asked: "What does woman want?" Maybe women are seen as mysterious by men because they don't express or even acknowledge their needs. Maybe if women came to know their needs more clearly, they would find the courage to ask for their needs to be met in a straightforward way. Then, not only would they please their partners, but they would feel more powerful in the world.

BECOMING SANTA CLAUS

Another important step toward using satya and right speech in our relationship is to be aware of our beliefs about our needs. If we believe that our needs are a burden to others, we will be reluctant to request that our needs be met. One way to live in truth is to be clear about what we would like. But the process of making clear requests has another layer of importance and meaning.

When we don't ask for what we want, it can reflect the unconscious belief that our needs are not important, or paradoxically that we are special or different from others and really don't need anything. This way of thinking is a form of egoism: we secretly believe that we are better than others, that our needs are minor or nonexistent, and therefore we don't need to ask others for support. Perhaps we have twisted the teachings of yoga or Buddhism to conclude that asking for support is selfish or demanding. But there is another way to be in the world.

Ike and I have learned from Marshall Rosenberg to ask this question of ourselves: What if we acted as if our requests to each other were actually giving a gift? What if you truly believed that you were not only giving your partner a gift but the best gift in the world by making a request? That gift is the opportunity for the other person to meet your needs. You are becoming Santa Claus, and they are getting a present! Believing that our needs are a burden is its own special hell. Believing that our needs are a gift is the way out of that hell.

We are not suggesting that just because you request that your need be met in a certain way that it will be. Rather, we are suggesting, first, that you can find the courage to ask, and second, that you can do so without whining or complaining. Making a request is a way of giving your partner the gift of being able to choose to give you what you want. And giving to the people we love, when it comes from deep in the heart, is one of life's greatest pleasures. If you ask from the place of "You lucky partner, you, I'm going to give you the chance to meet my needs," you have become Santa Claus.

However, if we ask for our partner to grant our request before we have expressed our feelings and needs, they will not have what they require to enjoy the process. We want to bring people to our needs first, then to our request. We want our partners to act from the belief that meeting our needs is the most wonderful thing they could be doing at the moment. There is never any demand energy around the request. When we give from that place, we shift, our partner shifts, and the world shifts toward compassion.

Imagine your partner coming to you and saying, "What can I say or do right now to make your life more wonderful?" I am guessing that you would melt with affection. The techniques of NVC are about creating the connection whereby we can all make life more wonderful for others. This helps us live the spirit of truth, and truth is rooted in love.

Please note that when we speak this way to each other, we are never doing anything *for* the other person. In fact, no one ever does anything for anyone. *We only do things to meet our own needs.* If we do anything for our partners for any other reason than to meet our own needs of contribution and support, then we are not truly giving a gift. That type of "gift" will have expectations and strings attached to it, usually unconscious ones. The other person will feel the hidden obligation. If we do anything out of "should" or "have to" energy, if there is even the slightest tinge of resentment or implied punishment for refusing to do it, we are doing violence to ourselves and to the relationship.

In the end, "self sacrifice" only makes others pay. This form of sacrifice can be driven by thoughts of duty or obligation, it can be an attempt to buy love in order to get people to like us, or it can be motivated by our desire to please God. If we act from these motivations, we suffer and we create suffering. Instead, if everything we do for others comes from the intention of meeting our own needs, everything is clear, and we live in the present.

DOGGING FOR YOUR NEEDS

Remember the duck index from chapter 4? Before you give to your partner, check in with your duck index. Give to them only when it is high on your index. Don't give up asking for your needs to be met just because you are met with resistance. Dog for your needs—have the persistence of a dog that continually comes back and slips his head under your hand so you will pet him. He does it with love.

Go to your partner and tell him what you need, and make a request. If your request is not granted, give yourself and your partner silent empathy and then ask again. And again. Ask from your heart, using slightly different strategies each time. This is not the same as nagging. Nagging is a form of demand; asking for needs to be met is a request. When we nag, we are in effect acting like the other person is at fault—we "blame" them for our emotional state and so expect them to "fix" us. Asking for our needs to be met takes responsibility for what we need and attempts to get it. So make sure that no criticism is implied or expressed. All criticism is the tragic expression of unmet needs. Never forget that your needs are a gift to you and a gift to your partner, because your needs are what connect you both directly to life.

FIGHTING ABOUT THE SAME THING OVER AND OVER

It seems to be a hallmark of long relationships that partners tend to have the same fight over and over again. Our fight is about temperature. One of us says, "It's cold in here," and the other one replies, "No, it isn't," and we are off to the races. Partners are often unable to resolve long-standing conflicts because when the disagreement arises, the people involved go immediately to strategies to solve the problem. We personally go to the tried-and-true, "Well, if you're cold, put on more clothes," while the other partner says, "No, if you're hot, take off some clothes." What works better is to use empathic connection around each person's feeling and needs, to make sure each person has been heard. When we feel heard, we become curious about what the other's needs are, and we are open to new strategies to meet all the needs that are up at the moment.

Marshall Rosenberg says he can help couples solve any long-standing disagreement within twenty minutes of the time that the couple have begun to hear each other's needs. Years of conflict gone in twenty minutes? The key is first giving and receiving empathy. He once asked an audience to say who among the couples there had the longest-standing disagreement. A couple spoke up who had argued about the checkbook for decades. It took quite a while for each partner, with his help, to hear the other's needs empathically, but when they did, they solved the problem of the checkbook in about ten minutes.

When I heard this story, I felt great hope and yet profound sadness. We all get stuck in repetitive arguments. For me it has never been about the "topic" of the fight; it has always been about the need for empathy. Learning to give and receive empathy with our partner opens doors of connection and love. We all are longing to be seen and heard, just for who we are, without judgments. Give that gift to your partner, and maybe you will transcend your most common fight. It's worth a try.

GOING UNCONSCIOUS

All spiritual practices are fundamentally about the same thing: being present and living with an open heart. It is the essence of living consciously. But in the hectic business of daily life and the habitual patterns of long relationships, almost of us "go unconscious" when our patterns are triggered by our partner or by circumstances.

It is worthwhile to spend some quiet time reflecting on what you do when you go unconscious in your relationship. Do you withdraw? Do you blame the other? Do you defend against all incoming statements because you hear them as criticism? Once you have found the basic thought and reaction you use habitually, share it with your partner. They will definitely recognize your pattern; they have been dancing with it for years. Then try this strategy.

Agree upon a signal that your partner can use to help you in your commitment to stay present in the midst of an upset. It might be a raised finger or a certain word that your partner can use to remind you that you are lapsing into your pattern. You can choose the same signal or individual ones. The important thing is that you use them.

Some years ago, Ike discussed with our family his habitual pattern of forgetting how much he valued staying present, and he asked for us all to help him notice when he was not doing that. Soon afterward, one night at dinner he became irritated and began to speak in a critical way. One of our children, then a young adult, remembered the mutual agreement Ike had made with us and said, "Dad, is this the way you want to interact? Is this the type of connection you want to have right now?" That was enough to remind Ike of his values and commitment to clarity in communication. He said he was going to leave the room, get centered, and return to connect in the way he wanted with his son. And he did so.

The rest of our evening was pleasant for everyone, as we celebrated our time together as a family. It was a breakthrough for all of us. We learned that we *can* change our patterns, if we remain aware of what we are doing. Ike's choices were our inspiration.

NEVER HEAR CRITICISM

When we lose connection with the intention behind what we say, especially with intimate partners, we find that we have a vast vocabulary for saying what is wrong with them. Some partners hear criticism no matter what we say. What is needed is emergency empathy.

Sometimes the most efficacious thing is to say something like, "I'm not able to hear you right now. I'm going for a walk until I can get centered, and then I'd like to try again to hear what your heart wants me to hear."

Never hear what the other person *thinks* of you. They may think that you caused their pain and may even use guilt to trick you into thinking that you did indeed cause it. You didn't. It is not what the other person said that caused my pain; it is how I chose to hear it.

You may have stimulated the other person, but they created their own pain by the way they heard you. So, instead of hearing what your partner *thinks,* hear what they are saying from their heart. Hear what is hidden in the words of criticism of you. Is the other person actually hurt, afraid, or frustrated? Give yourself and them silent empathy. Do not go to solution or strategy until you both have shifted.

One of the most pungent things we have learned from Dr. Rosenberg is that in relationships we are all "becoming progressively less stupid." Hopefully the relationship can withstand the strain until we begin to figure out how we trigger each other and which specific words do that. Then we can give and receive empathy to create connection and ease, at least until the next time.

One strategy that can strengthen connection is to consistently celebrate how the other person is enriching your life. Build that celebration into your relationship structure;

create a space to do it every day. One way might be to offer appreciation to your partner for something she does every day. For example, "I really appreciate you getting up early and going to work so we can live in this house," or "Thank you for fixing this dinner. I know it took time and effort, and I want you to know that I enjoy the tastes and trust in its wholesomeness."

THE MYTH OF INDEPENDENCE

Most of us are raised to think it is important to be independent, to think for ourselves, to make up our own minds about things. Partly because of these cultural norms, we are not clear about the distinctions between dependence and independence, and therefore we miss the joy of interdependence.

To be dependent is to believe and act from the idea that only a specific other person can meet my needs—for example, my need for love. I might say something like, "I need you to love me." Actually this statement is a strategy. If we believe that in order to get love, we must get it from that specific person, then we are dependent on that person. So unless that person gives us love, or we can persuade, manipulate, or cajole them into loving us, we will not have love in life. That is a scary place to be.

To protect ourselves from this dependency and from potential hurt, sometimes we act and speak from the belief that we are completely independent of others. This way of looking at the world reinforces the idea that no one can meet our needs except ourselves. This may seem like a safer place to be, but it is a lonely place.

There is a third way to act and speak. It is to use your speech to acknowledge the interdependence we have with other people. Interdependence means that my needs cannot be met unless yours are, and yours cannot be met unless mine are. With this awareness, it becomes clear that needs, the human needs we all have, are what connect us to each other.

No relationship will thrive and be healthy unless both people are getting their needs met. This includes the relationships of boss and employee, husband and wife, teacher and student, and friends. A relationship cannot survive in which one person is consistently getting what they need and the other one is not.

HOW TO ENJOY SCREWING THINGS UP

One of the things that often holds us back when we begin to use NVC with our partners is the fear of making a mess. Our advice is to go ahead and make a mess without fear. Then you can use your newly acquired NVC skills to clean up the mess. Relax with confidence in your ability to mourn your "mistakes" with your partner and to try again to create connection.

PRACTICING NONVIOLENT COMMUNICATION

Making life more wonderful

- Make a plan with your partner that every day for the next week, when you wake up, the first thing you will ask each other is "What can I do to contribute to your day being more wonderful?" Notice what fun this is to do. Be sure to follow through with empathic listening to the response and with the requested action, if it is at least a 6 on your duck index.
- At the end of the day, acknowledge out loud to your partner your gratitude for what they did to make your life more wonderful today.

Intentional guessing

- Spend ten minutes with your partner, and have them tell you about a recent incident (not involving you) in which they were upset. Help them recall what feelings and needs came up for them at the time. Then support them to say how they are feeling and what they are needing in the present moment, as they recall the incident. Do not offer solutions, just empathy.
- When it feels comfortable, try this same exercise with an incident that does include you and your partner.

7

TALKING TO OUR CHILDREN AND PARENTS

Telling someone what was wrong with them never got me what I wanted from them.

—MARSHALL ROSENBERG

A FEW YEARS into our study of NVC, we were having a discussion with our teenage daughter. Apparently our skill level was still elementary, because when we tried to use NVC in our conversation, she replied: "I have no feelings, needs, or requests, so stop using that NVC stuff on me. I know what you're doing." Because of our lack of experience, we were effectively stymied by her response. Indeed, learning to communicate in a new way with our children and parents is probably one of the most difficult areas in which to use the principles of spiritual speech.

Perhaps one of the reasons that the child–parent relationship is challenging is that it has to do with shifting power. When children are born, we as parents seem to have all the power. Gradually, as they grow, we surrender more and more choices to them, until they leave home and live their own lives. But often parents hold the unconscious belief that they are in charge of their children, of what they say, do, and believe.

The opposite happens in the relationship with our parents. When we visit our parents, or if they have passed and we think of them, there sometimes arises the old rebellious spirit. We may feel slightly irritated in their presence if we perceive that they are judging our choices or trying to tell us what to do or offering advice. We want them to back off and treat us as the adults we believe we have become, even if we are only fifteen years old at the time.

POWER OVER OR POWER WITH

Marshall Rosenberg relates that his relationship with his children shifted dramatically when he realized he could not make his children do anything—he could just make them wish they had. When he operated this way, though, he found out that they would make him wish he hadn't made them wish they had. So goes the world, when we operate from the paradigm of "power over."

As young parents, Ike and I believed that parenting was not only about loving our children, but it was also about making them mind us and act in certain ways. We believed that was what responsible parents did. There is only one problem with acting from this belief: It is a short-term solution, and it has consequences you may not like. It is possible at times to get your child to do what you want by using your power as a parent. But there is no way that using power can force your child to do something for the reasons you want them to do it. Unless we can find other ways to connect and communicate, we will be building child–parent relationships that not only aren't satisfying but that are filled with suffering for both child and parent.

Ike and I quickly found out with our first child that we couldn't even control a two-year-old. We could put him in his room because he was having a temper tantrum and tell him to stay, but we couldn't make him like it or stop trying to come out. It was quite humbling.

Here is where speech as a spiritual practice comes in. Suzuki Roshi said, when asked about controlling teenagers, "You cannot control their behavior, you can only control your own." This makes it clear that a regular practice of self-awareness, like yoga or meditation, can help us as parents be clear about what is alive in us and what our needs are exactly. It can help us be a little more discriminating about what is in our power to change and what is not. Finally, self-awareness practices can help us to see our child as an individual and to separate clearly what are our needs and what are theirs.

I (Judith) once heard a child psychologist say that when your child is facing a difficulty, ask yourself: Is it my problem as a parent, is it the child's problem, or is it a problem for both of us to solve? He suggested that if it is your problem, you get help for it. If it is your child's problem, you support them in solving it. If it is a problem for both of you, you figure out a way to solve it together. The difficult part is discriminating whose problem it is.

It is very easy to want to do everything for our children to protect them. There is even a term for this: helicopter parent. This is the type who hovers over every activity and every aspect of their child's life, like a helicopter. It is really the manifestation of attempting to have power over the child's life and choices. It may come from desperately wanting to make the child's life happy, healthy, and safe, but it has consequences.

By learning NVC, we have shifted our understanding of power in human relationships. We learned that what we wanted was power *with* our children, not power *over*. This does not mean that we give up our role as their parents; rather it means that we understand that all human beings have power, even in the most constrained circumstances. If someone points a gun at your head and says,

"Your money or your life," you may not like that choice, but you still have the power to make one.

Children, even young children, have choice about their feelings and their thoughts. They may do what we want on the outside, but they will do what they want on the inside. The most successful relationships with children are based on recognizing that they also have power. This does not mean that we give up our responsibility to protect and guide, but rather that we understand that they are part of the process. If you don't believe this, try to use your power to "make" a teenager do well in school. Let us know how it goes! They will do what they will. We can only choose our own actions. If our language does not reflect this, then we are not living in reality.

We learned in NVC that we had been acting as if we had power over our children. To act from the belief of power over is to attempt to use words or actions to get someone to do what you want them to. There is an implicit use of force behind the words if the other does not comply. If you want to see what kind of world this belief creates, look around. Even with all the progress human society has made, we often attempt to solve problems by the use of power over.

Power with, on the other hand, uses communication skills to recognize each person's power and to come to a mutually acceptable solution to problems in which all the people in the situation have their needs met.

Two examples of how we learned about the use of power with our children might be useful here. One instance was when our thirteen-year-old daughter and her friend proposed going to a rock concert and "staying out till 2 a.m." When she initially asked, my silent reaction was "in your dreams!" But recognizing that she was taller than me and could walk out the door and I would never again see her (or any potential grandchildren), and furthermore acknowledging that I was not going to chain her to her bed, I realized that my best strategy was to negotiate. I used my favorite parenting mantra: "Oh, tell me more." This is an effective tactic that gives you time to breathe and consider the situation. I got clear during this pause that I really didn't care about her going with her friend to the rock concert, but I really cared about her being safe.

As she continued to enthuse about the groups and the music, I remembered my NVC. I said, "I hear that you're excited about the concert, but I have some concerns. Would you like to spend ten minutes now brainstorming ways that we could both get our needs met in this situation?" This type of approach acknowledges the other person's needs and passions. The other person feels heard and is then more willing to hear you and your needs.

When she agreed to continue the discussion on the needs level, I told her that my needs were all about her safety. I said that I had three strategies that would meet my need for safety and that I was guessing would also meet her needs for adventure and fun. I suggested them one by one, and she agreed to them all. These strategies were that her older and very trustworthy brother accompany them, that he stay with them so they were not roaming unaccompanied in the crowd, and that she be home by midnight.

Not only was all this agreeable to her, but we ended the discussion with a sense of connection and celebration instead of the argument that so often happens when teenagers push the envelope and parents react with fear and power plays. The most interesting thing about the whole situation was that she came home from the concert at 10 p.m. because it was too loud. She felt free to make the choice to meet her needs. She didn't need to prove anything to me by rebelling.

Another example involved our nineteen-year-old son. He was driving alone to a ski area to join another young man who we knew, for a few days of snowboarding. As he was leaving, I tried to force an agreement from him about calling me from the road and when he arrived. He balked, and I upped the ante. "No," I said, "call me every day, just call me all the time! Never stop calling me!" I was feeling the need for reassurance and connection, and he was feeling the need for adventure and autonomy. His response, famous in the annals of teen and parent relationships was, "You don't trust me!"

Thank goodness Ike gently intervened and lent us his NVC skills. He helped our son and me get clear about our respective needs. When my son heard that me wanting "lots of phone calls" was a strategy to meet my needs for safety and reassurance, he relaxed because *it was about me and was not an implied criticism*. He began to understand that it was not about me trusting him. And when he demonstrated with words that he heard me, I relaxed and was able to hear his needs for autonomy and adventure.

When we finally heard each other's needs, we were able to agree on a phone call strategy that met both of our needs. Ironically, by the third day of the trip, I asked him to stop calling me so much, because I was content with our connection. The few minutes we had spent getting clear on our needs through NVC were about each of us paying attention first to what was alive in ourselves, then to what we really needed, and finally to being willing to let go of our respective expectations (strategies), so we could be open to outcome.

The situation resolved with connection and both of us getting our needs met. It was a great learning experience for me. Once again, I saw that power with my children was what I wanted, not power over them, because power with them helped to create the kind of relationship I wanted to have.

PROTECTIVE USE OF FORCE

NVC, as well as yoga philosophy and Buddhism, holds dear the values of nonviolence. NVC offers the additional teaching of the protective use of force. The protective use of force means using just the force necessary to prevent someone from harming themselves or others. That force is applied with compassion and not anger, and it is never used to punish.

It is occasionally necessary to use force to protect or save lives. If my child were in the street, I would not stop and have an NVC conversation with a three-year-old about the danger of an oncoming truck. I would grab the child and run to safety. To use NVC does not imply that we surrender our protective urges as parents, or that we give in or give up our parenting responsibilities. Rather it helps us realize that most of the decisions we make regarding our children are not about life-threatening situations, and that valuing and using the tool of mutuality can make the relationship deeper and more satisfying.

A famous story from India beautifully expresses the concept of the protective use of force. A sadhu was making his yearly circuit around the villages in India. In one village, after lecturing on *ahimsa*, nonviolence, he encountered a large and aggressive snake. The snake had been terrorizing the village, but it listened intently to the teachings of the sadhu regarding nonviolence.

A year passed, and the wandering sadhu returned to the village to find the snake hiding in the bushes, skinny, battered, and bruised. When asked what had happened to him, the snake replied that he had taken the teachings of ahimsa to heart and no longer threatened anyone. The children quickly learned that the snake was not a threat and taunted and threw rocks at him. The snake was no longer able to find food and was near death.

The sadhu responded, "Yes, I did teach you to practice nonviolence, but I never told you not to hiss." Using protective force with our children, or anyone else for that matter, is remembering to hiss when necessary.

AUTONOMY, AUTONOMY, AUTONOMY

One of the reasons that power over does not give us what we want is that it does not recognize or respect the fundamental requirement for a good relationship: respect for the other's autonomy. A definition of *child* or *teenager* or *young adult* might be "a person who wants you to respect their autonomy." The closer you are to the person, the more desperately they want you to respect their autonomy.

The first sign of rebellion in the child–parent relationship is often termed the terrible twos. We never understood what was so terrible about this stage of development until we were in the midst of it with our firstborn. It wasn't so terrible for him, but it was pretty terrible for us. It was the age of No! On every occasion throughout his day, for several months, he made it clear that we needed to respect his autonomy. He wanted to make the decision about when he got into the car seat and if and when he got out. He wanted to be in charge of whether he got into the bathtub and if and when he got out. He wanted to decide when he went to sleep. Child experts tell us this is a normal stage of human development. That doesn't help. I'm not sure which is more unpleasant—hearing No! all day long or witnessing the death of the illusion that we as parents have all the power.

A fascinating example of the mutuality of power between parent and child can be seen in a movie called *One Fine Day*. The scene involves the dad (George Clooney) and his approximately eight-year-old daughter. She is under a table, clutching a kitten she passionately wants to keep, and her dad is under the table with her, just as passionately wanting her to come with him because he has a tight schedule. He tries using power over her, he tries using bribery, but nothing works until he finally begins to listen to her needs. When she feels heard, both her needs and his can be met, and she goes with him willingly. While they are not using formal NVC language, they are definitely using colloquial NVC and the spirit of mutuality.

WHAT WE WANT FROM OUR PARENTS

Probably the thing we want most from our parents is their unconditional love. But following close on its heels is the desire for them to recognize and respect our autonomy. This doesn't seem to go away, even into adulthood.

As we grow up, we may feel the need to demand respect for our autonomy, and we may choose one of several strategies to get that respect. One strategy is to rebel. This is a simple and almost universal strategy: "I want X, my parents want Y, so I will do X, even though I see that Y is a better idea, because no one is going tell me what to do." This scenario is acted out daily in many homes. Sometimes the rebellion is overt and sometimes it is sneaky, but the war is on.

Another strategy is to just give up and submit to the authority of our parents. This approach can breed seething anger and hidden rebellion. It sometimes occurs in homes where rebellion may not be perceived as safe by the child, because of situations like alcoholism or abuse.

Most of us stumble through to adulthood without a clear understanding of mutuality and shared power with our parents. We may run companies, hire and fire employees, buy and sell homes, write books, and become parents ourselves, but with our parents we can still be stimulated into defending our need for respect for our autonomy.

When you find yourself in this position with your parents or grandparents, NVC would suggest that you first give yourself silent empathy for the sadness or irritation that arises when you hear your parent act in a way that does not respect your autonomy. You may need to do self-empathy frequently when you are in their presence.

You might also arrange to receive some out-loud empathy from a friend before you visit or talk with your parents. Once you are feeling full, your natural curiosity will arise about what might be alive in your parents, and you can shift to giving them empathy. When we can empathize, there is nothing to forgive, and old hurts and fears seem less important.

A final approach to create and maintain connection with your parents is to express your need and ask for specific things in return. You might say that you want to improve your communication and then guess their feelings and needs about a specific issue. Be willing to keep trying, time and again, and never stop giving yourself empathy.

WHY APPROVAL HURTS

As parents we sometimes use our approval and praise to reward and manipulate our children. This strategy to get our needs met may seem loving, but it has problems inherent in it. When we offer approval, compliments, or praise, we are telling the other person that we like them or what they did by using evaluative language. This is to offer them our judgments, even though those judgments are usually considered to be "positive."

The problem is that implied in the praise is the unexpressed understanding that if the person did well, he could also do badly. If you look beautiful, you could also look ugly. If I put you on the "beautiful" continuum in my mind, the other end of that continuum is "ugly." Praise and compliments put your child, or any other person, in a box. It tells them who they are and therefore limits them. Think back to a time when someone gave you a compliment and you felt uneasy. Your discomfort was possibly because the compliment, even if positive, implied the possibility of its opposite.

Compliments and praise focus on extrinsic rewards. In *Punished by Rewards*, author Alfie Kohn cites various studies that show that not only do praise and rewards fail to create the desired ends, they actually cause the desired behavior to decrease. So the long-term effect of attempting to manipulate your child or others with praise and compliments is counterproductive.

Instead of offering praise and compliments, *appreciate* your children. In NVC this means to share with others exactly what they said or did that met your specific needs. So instead of saying, "You are a good boy for washing the dishes," you might say, "When I came home and saw the clean kitchen, my needs for help and support were met. Thank you."

When we offer appreciation, we not only avoid judging others, we also reveal what contributes to our happiness and well-being. When we use NVC appreciation, we give the gift of showing another how their actions contributed to our well-being, which Marshall Rosenberg calls "the best game in town." Not only do we feel better appreciating instead of rewarding, but it has the additional advantage of connecting us to ourselves, to the other person, and to the moment. This is spiritual speech in daily life.

PRACTICING NONVIOLENT COMMUNICATION

Learning about power over

- Pay attention to the language you hear on television or the radio for the next few days. Notice how often people use words that express power over others.

- Notice the next time you use words that express power over. When you can, spend some quiet time alone, connecting with how those words were stimulated at that moment by you feeling powerless.

Offering appreciation

- Make a commitment to express appreciation to each of your family members once a day for a week.
- In the next conversation you have with your parents, whether on the phone or in person or in your mind, offer yourself empathy when you become agitated or upset.

8

TALKING AT WORK

Focus on what you want, not on what you fear.

—IKE LASATER

WHEN I FIRST started taking workshops with Marshall, I (Ike) was in the midst of litigating a complicated, multiparty environmental case in federal court. At the beginning of the trial, the counsel for all parties jointly agreed to a tentative estimate of a two-week trial length. Toward the beginning of the fourth week of the trial, I was in the midst of cross-examining a well-qualified chemist who was a witness for the government. I had taken her deposition and, given that I knew her testimony well, I wanted to highlight particular parts of it to make sure it got into the court record. Since her primary testimony was more favorable to the government, I asked her questions that would guide her toward what my client would find as more desirable answers during my cross-examination.

Over and over again, this is how it would go: She would answer my question. Then, she would qualify what she just said by unnecessarily restating what she'd already testified to, the result of which was doubling or tripling the time for her testimony. We were two weeks behind schedule and had three witnesses still to go, and the chemist's inexperience was delaying us unnecessarily. It was an excruciating process.

In my frustration, I began to use the standard cross-examination techniques and strategies to "control" witnesses. They did not work. What's more, at one of the breaks, the chemist told my female associates that she thought I was a "sexist pig" who was trying to control and demean her. Even though it upset me to hear this, it did not occur to me that there was any other way to communicate with her.

Day one ended. The court scheduled my cross-examination to continue the next day; however, I was concerned that if the process continued the way it had gone thus far, the judge would cut off the testimony. I would not get what I wanted into the record. The situation was a mess. As I walked back to my hotel, I tried to figure out what to do. A voice in my head said, *Why don't you try NVC?* The immediate response? *No way, you can't use NVC in the courtroom in front of opposing counsel, standing before a federal judge.*

Still, I started to think about using the language I had begun to experiment with in the world of NVC. I imagined the worst-case scenario using these words in the stilted, formal environment of a federal courthouse: me at a podium twenty feet from the witness box and government lawyers poised to object to anything I did that deviated from what they expected. Still, I imagined scenarios in which I used the words I practiced in Marshall's workshops. It scared and excited me at the same time.

The following day, I picked up my cross-examination where we had left off. I asked my first question, and much as I expected, the chemist behaved just as she had the day before. She answered my question, then, just as she started to restate what she testified for the government, I took a deep breath and interrupted, "Excuse me." Surprised, she stopped. I had her attention. "I'm worried about the time it's taking to complete your testimony. I'm wondering if you'd be willing just to answer my questions first and save any extra explanation until the end. I want to assure you that you will have time to talk to government counsel before your testimony is complete, and you'll be able to explain things further if you need to. Would you be willing, for now, to just answer my questions?" I watched the chemist, and I could see her body language relax. Still, as I spoke, I could feel my heart rate skyrocket. Irrationally, I worried that one of the opposing attorneys was going to jump up and object, "You can't use NVC in the courtroom!" Of course, that didn't happen, and after getting an OK nod from the government counsel, the chemist said yes to my request.

Though I did have to remind her of our agreement a couple of times, she soon self-corrected and answered my questions without restating the testimony she had given for the government. The cross-examination proceeded much more quickly, and I got the testimony I wanted into the court record. To my amazement, using NVC in the "real world" had been a success.

PREPARING YOURSELF

If the thought of using NVC at work gives you butterflies in your stomach, my story shows you you're not alone. Rest assured, many others have faced similar fears and, like me, have overcome them. If you'd like to try to use NVC in your work life, I suggest you begin by imagining the worst fears this scenario invokes for you. Or, in NVC terms, name the needs you imagine will not be met if you use NVC in this environment. Just naming those needs is a way to bring back the present moment and often shift you to a calm, more at ease state.

I have found that practice is indispensable for the quality of your NVC skill and reduces the apprehension you may feel at bringing NVC into the workplace. To that end, try to find people you trust to practice with *before* you are in that setting so that you can rehearse scenarios that are related to your work.

PRACTICING WITH A FRIEND

One way to prepare yourself is to practice your newly acquired NVC skills with a friend. To do so, I suggest you make an agreement with this person. This agreement could sound something like this: "I've recently been studying something called Nonviolent Communication. It's an approach based on the notion that all humans share the same basic needs, and that each of our actions is a strategy to meet one or more of these needs. I'd like to try some of the things that I've been learning with you. If you agree, keep in mind the vocabulary you hear may sound unusual. If you feel uncomfortable with it for any reason and at any point and you don't want me to continue, please, will you agree to stop me? Then we can talk about it, and I won't try to keep practicing with you. Are you willing to try what I've proposed?" If your friend or loved one agrees, this is a way for you to become more at ease with this new way of thinking, behaving, and speaking, and this new ease will help you once you are using your NVC skills "in the wild."

BABY STEPS: SELF-EMPATHY AND SILENT EMPATHY

Another way to prepare yourself to use NVC in the workplace is to practice silently until you feel confident about doing your work orally with this person. You can take these "baby steps" by incorporating NVC at work in a way that won't be obvious to others, such as using self-empathy and silent empathy.

As a reminder, when you practice self-empathy, you connect with your own (met or unmet) needs, and when you practice silent empathy, you guess other people's needs. If, for instance, you were having a difficult conversation with a colleague at work, you can practice self- or silent empathy in the moment, or you can practice later when you have a chance to reflect. This might happen, for instance, while you are on your commute home after work. You can reflect upon which of your needs were not met and which were met by what went on during your day. For instance:

Observation: What are you saying to yourself? What did you say that prompted you to have this internal dialogue of self-criticism, or what did the other person say that prompted your inner dialogue of criticism for them?

Feeling: Identify how you feel when you recall the observation, bringing it into consciousness. How does that memory prompt you to feel?

Need: Determine *in this moment* if your need is met or not met—not while you were experiencing the event in the past, but while you're doing the reflecting.

Request: Do you have a request for yourself or the other person? Your request for the other person might be to ask them to sit down and talk to you about the conversation, while your request for yourself might be to practice with somebody to prepare for the next conversation.

TAKING THE LEAP

While silent practices and role-playing can help you increase your skills and ease you into using NVC, you also might simply decide to start using it. Julie Greene, an NVC trainer, once told me that at a certain point, she decided she was going to "jump off the cliff" and use NVC in all her interactions. She realized that she would create many "messes" with people in doing this, but she'd use those messes as learning opportunities. What I think she meant is that to those familiar with her usual way of speaking, this new language might seem not only strange and unusual but also *unnatural*. When this disconnection inevitably occurred, she used her newfound skills to reestablish connection with her friend or acquaintance. And thus, it set in motion a perpetual learning process.

After Julie told me this anecdote, I put my fear to the side, stepped off my own metaphoric cliff, and embraced the messes I knew I was about to make by practicing NVC in the workplace.

MAKING REQUESTS

Very often, we don't feel safe enough at work to ask people for what we want. There are many reasons for this. One may be that because we believe that a person has power over us, we think we're not in a position to ask for a change, and we do not check our assumptions. Our needs for safety and security then get in the way of approaching that person we perceive to hold that power. It's a self-defeating process: we feel our needs are not being met, yet we don't make the very request that might meet our needs.

Let's use this scenario as an example, carved from the year of COVID-19 when so many employees across the globe found themselves in a conflagration fueled by stressors at work and home. A 2020 report by McKinsey ("Diverse Employees are Struggling the Most during COVID-19—Here's How Companies Can Respond," November 17, 2020) examined data based on surveys and interviews with

"Diverse" employees (identified as women, LGBTQ+, people of color, and working parents) in eleven developed and developing countries across the globe. It called attention to the fact that diverse employees struggled the most in their workplace environments during the COVID-19 crisis. Women who worked, especially women of color, faced an extraordinarily high amount of stress.

In this imagined request scenario, a working mother struggles to work efficiently from home while her children attend school remotely. At the same time, she is "competing" with other colleagues for a promotion, colleagues who do not fall into the "Diverse" category. She decides to have a conversation with the head of her department to express her concern and, at the same time, request that she have more flexibility in terms of when she gets her work done. She would also like to ask him for reassurance that the circumstances won't affect his consideration for the promotion. In this scenario, this is how I suggest practicing at home with a friend before making the request in person with the head of the department.

1. Identify the need that is not being met in the situation until you feel the physiological shift in your body that says you have connected with it.
2. With the clarity of your need in mind, identify for yourself what you want in this situation.

3. With what you want in mind, turn your attention to crafting your request.
4. Role-play making that request and having the other person play your department head while giving you the response you fear receiving.
5. Provide yourself with empathy and practice how you would like to respond.

As you develop more skill in making requests, you'll probably start to notice that your colleagues rarely make direct requests. You can begin to lend your skills to others to help them make explicit, doable requests. For example, suppose you are in a meeting, and someone has been talking for a bit without making it clear what they want. In that case, you might interject and say, "Excuse me, Jeremy; it would be so helpful to me if you would tell me what you would like me to do with the information you've shared over the last few minutes. Would you tell me so that I can better organize my notes?" This approach has the added benefit of helping the person who is speaking to clarify their request.

GUESSING WHAT PEOPLE WANT

Another option in the situation I described above would be to guess what the other person might want. You could say, "Hey Jeremy, is this discussion about how you want us to agree on a strategy?" Your guess may be incorrect, but again it will prompt the person to speak to tell you what they want. Helping your colleagues reach this kind of clarity is beneficial for the whole team.

In our personal lives, we often make a request directly to one person, perhaps our partner or child, but in the workplace, we are more likely to be in group situations. If you are in a meeting or speaking to your team, you must be clear about your request and *to whom it is directed*. If your team doesn't know you are talking to them, then no agreement can be made. And your words are, therefore, likely to create confusion.

Often in groups, people make demands that are motivated by their frustration with what is happening in the room (virtual or in person). I'm sure most of us have either been that person irritated by what is going on or witnessed someone else's angry outburst. But when you speak out of anger, impatience, or irritation, your colleagues tend to dismiss what you've said, saying something like, "You're just arguing. Let's get on with the real business here." I've seen variations of this again and again over the years.

Because these outbursts are motivated by frustration and not by a connection to needs, they have the exact opposite effect on the person who makes the outburst. The expression of frustration often triggers others to express their *own* irritation, which delays the conversation even further. There is an alternative.

INTERRUPTING NEEDS

At a conference I once attended, a general session took place with about forty-five people in attendance. The facilitator asked the audience for information to help him better understand a situation related to the conference topic. Many people eagerly raised their hands and began to give their opinions. Soon, a heated argument developed among a number of the participants, all of whom were senior members of the professional community attending the conference. This debate went on and on for about fifteen minutes, with the people involved getting more and more invested in their viewpoints while the rest of us still waited to return to the planned schedule for the session.

I felt as I imagine many of my fellow attendees felt: frustrated that this arguing was wasting our time and annoyed that the facilitator wasn't taking charge and getting the session back on track. This wasn't what I paid for, not what I had been looking forward to, and not where I wanted to be.

Then I took a breath and remembered my NVC training.

The first thing I did was practice self-empathy. I looked for observational language for what people were saying or doing that was stimulating all these feelings. I asked, *Which of my needs are* not *being met by what's going on?*

This practice was very constructive, as it created a kind of openness in me, a space that resulted from stepping outside of my judgments about the situation.

I then began to look for strategies: What could I do to help in this situation that would both meet my needs and help other people in the room?

I had an idea. I stood up and said, "Excuse me, I'm uncomfortable with what's going on here." This generated some laughter, as I don't think people were used to hearing someone talk about their feelings in this setting. "I want to understand what's going on and whether this is answering the facilitator's question." I turned to the facilitator. "My request is: Are you willing to tell us, of all that has been said in response to your question, what has been helpful?" He looked stunned. After a long pause, he said, "None of it has been responsive to my question, except for what this person said over here." He looked at someone sitting off to the side.

The comment he was referring to had come relatively soon after he posed the question and was not at all on the argument's topic.

The room seemed to shift after that. The argument stopped, and the conversation changed to the one thing the facilitator said he had found valuable. I enjoyed the ensuing discussion and found it helpful.

The shift did not occur because of my position in this community; at the time, I was one of the junior members. I believe the shift took place because I used NVC to step outside of my judgments, get clear on my needs, and formulate a request that would help create what I wanted. My request cut through people's investment in their viewpoints and judgments of other people and returned the group to its original intention—an answer to the facilitator's question.

It is only when we step outside of our analyses or evaluations of what's happening and connect with our needs that we can formulate the kind of request that I formulated. If I hadn't first practiced self-empathy to connect with my needs, and silent empathy to connect with the needs of others in the group, my question would have more likely sounded like, "Will people just shut up and move on to another topic?!" When we are not connected with ourselves, we often act in ways that create precisely what we don't want.

SILENTLY CONTRIBUTING TO A GROUP

When we are in group situations, we tend to think we always have to be outwardly doing something to contribute. Ironically, I often find that one of the most powerful ways to contribute is to do nothing outwardly but instead to focus on connecting inwardly with my own and others' needs. Even if you are in a group situation where you don't feel comfortable speaking up, you can contribute beneficially and change the meeting's dynamic by practicing self-empathy and silent empathy.

When you are just beginning to learn NVC, you might want to carry a notepad with you and do self-empathy on the pad. Jot down observations— "Joe's been talking for three minutes on this topic"—and then identify and write down your feeling and need. When you are clear on those, see if you have a request of yourself or someone else in the group, and write that down. This writing practice informs whether you say anything in the group. Writing it down instead of trying to do it in your head might focus you more, and even if you cannot come up with all four components mentioned earlier, it can help you shift away from dwelling on the same old thoughts of irritation and distress. This practice shifts our being, and anything we decide to do will come from a different energy, one more likely to align with our value of "right speech."

"EFFICIENT" COMMUNICATION

One of the primary benefits of using self-empathy and internally clarifying a request before making it is that it reduces the number of words we use. It's interesting that "efficiency" is one of the workplace buzzwords, yet often the concept is not extended to our communication with others. I hear people complain of interminable meetings, far too many emails containing far too many words, and irrelevant or redundant memos or voicemails. For the most part, we are not economical in our use of words. Using NVC as a model to practice right speech has the beneficial side effect of increasing our communications efficiency. We can get across the essential information in a way that connects us with others, using fewer words.

People sometimes seem to talk in order to figure out what they want to say, rather than figuring it out before they speak. You might find yourself in workplace situations where someone uses more words than you as a listener want to hear. It may be more words than the speaker wants, as well. I still have the residue of a habit in which I talk more if I feel the person I am speaking to is not present with what I am saying. This generally creates the opposite of what I want; the person becomes even *less* present, and I become even more frustrated.

You can help yourself and others increase the efficiency of your communication in several ways. If someone is talking more than you can take in, you can interrupt them with a question designed to help them get across what they want to say in fewer words. If you're going to say something, it helps to check with others to see if they are willing to hear what you have to say.

Often in meetings, we look for a gap in conversation and burst into that gap to try to get our point across, desperate to be heard. Sometimes we don't even wait for that gap; we cut off the last few words of the person speaking to get in our piece. But if I interrupt the person who is speaking to interject with what I have to say, in all likelihood, they won't listen to what I have to say.

I increase the likelihood that I'll be heard by first making sure that the person I am speaking to understands that I have heard what they are trying to communicate to me. Once they know that, I find their mind quiets, and they are open to listening to what I want to share. That openness increases if I check with them to see if they are willing to hear my perspective. I might say, "I'd like to tell you how I'm viewing that; are you willing to listen now?" If I'm genuinely requesting and not demanding ("Listen to me because I listened to you!"), then they are at choice, and if they say yes, it increases the likelihood that I'll be heard in the way I would like. I suspect that the person will be more present, and I can use fewer words to get my point across. If I want to check whether they've heard what I want them to hear or how they feel about it, I can use one of the process requests that we have discussed.

EMAILS AND TELEPHONE CALLS

Email and the telephone are two other communication areas where efficiency can be lacking. Many people face the daily task of sorting through more emails than they can answer and reading emails that are longer than they enjoy. Reading and writing emails at work can be another component of the practice of right speech. In reading the email, you can look for the four components of NVC, particularly needs and requests. If you are part of a work team where it is the custom to copy everybody on everything, this can help you know when you need to pay close attention and when you can file the email because the request is for someone else. If you find yourself irritated or dissatisfied, connect with your own unmet need that generated the irritation. Then, guess what need the sender was seeking to meet when they wrote the email to help you be more connected with what they wrote.

If the email request is unclear, I find it helpful to seek clarification from the sender. Just as in a meeting, getting this clarification ends up helping both you and the sender. Personally, it reduces my anxiety because when it's clear what the person wants, I feel freer to say whether I'm willing to do it or not, and if not, to amend the request in a way that I hope will satisfy us both.

Using NVC as a model for practicing the right speech works for *writing* emails as well. I have practiced by writing emails that are strictly structured along the lines of my observation, feelings about the situation, the needs I'm hoping to meet by sending the email, and an explicit request. Then I rewrite the email in more colloquial language while maintaining the clarity of the distinctions I made in the first writing. When I was first doing this practice, I found that if I tried to write colloquially without first going through the practice of making the clear distinctions, I would embed a series of judgments and conflate needs and strategies in a way that produced results I didn't like from the people I was addressing.

Telephone conversations are a large part of most people's work life, and all aspects of spoken communication apply; an additional component involves leaving voicemail messages. My practice with phone calls is similar to emails. I identify ahead of time my request of the person and what information I want from them to help them fulfill it. As always, doing this exercise dramatically increases the efficiency of my communication. I use far fewer words, which I think is welcomed by those listening; I certainly appreciate brevity when receiving voicemail messages. I also tend to order the information in a voicemail differently when I think ahead. I am likely to state my request initially, followed by enough data to support the person's desire to agree to it. Suppose I need some information from a colleague to complete a proposal we are jointly working on, for instance. In that case, I might leave a message saying, "Would you be willing to call me back by the end of today with the information on _____ so I can finish the proposal?"

GIVING EVALUATIONS

Another reality of many people's work lives is being evaluated on their work and, if you are a manager, assessing other people's work. Most evaluations use a scale applied to a series of judgments or labels, such as communication skills, teamwork, promptness in accomplishing work, and quality of work. Most of the evaluations I've seen conducted are inherently judgmental. Yet, they are usually couched in purportedly *objective* terms, making it difficult to know how to respond or what to do with the information. Evaluations often bring up complicated feelings tied to needs for sustainability, competence, and being understood and accepted. Assuming you cannot change the evaluation system at your workplace, how can you make evaluations more satisfying and helpful?

Since evaluations tie to judgments about a person's actions, the key to making them more practical and less problematic is to connect them to *observations*. If you evaluate someone else's performance, you can give examples in the observation language of each area you are evaluating. If, for instance, you rated someone highly on teamwork, you could give them the specific cases in which you saw them collaborate in ways you liked. Perhaps you ranked them lower on the promptness of completing work, in which case you would note the three times in the last quarter when they handed in reports past the time you had anticipated receiving the reports. In making the observation, you can tie it directly to needs and make a specific request regarding improvement in that area.

If someone else evaluates you, you can lend them your skills by asking them for the specific observations that would help you understand what led them to evaluate you as they did. If you are not clear on what needs of theirs are or are not met by some of the evaluation categories, you might instigate a discussion about it with them. Essentially this process translates the evaluation schema into observations and needs met or not met. And if your evaluator suggests areas of improvement but does not know how to make the requests, you can again lend your skills and translate what they say into request language.

GOSSIP

Gossip is a common feature of the workplace. Gathering at the watercooler or in the lunchroom, people lower their voices to pass along a tasty tidbit they heard about someone or share a story of what someone else did to them. Gossip is a social norm in many places, so avoiding it can be difficult, yet it is central to the Buddhist view of right speech and the yoga teaching of *satya*.

I find it helpful to define what I think is going on when people gossip. I see two different types of gossip that serve distinct purposes. One type serves as a mechanism for developing a shared set of norms. We tell stories about other people embedded with our judgments of their conduct, and we seek agreement from the people we are telling the story to, or at least we want to see if they share our norms.

In the other type of gossip, we tell a story that happened to us as a way to meet our need for empathy. Our story of an interaction with another person expresses our dissatisfaction through our judgments of that person's conduct. We want the person listening to conspire that we are right and the person we are talking about is wrong. The underlying dynamic here is our desire for someone to understand our distress and see our pain. If the other person agrees with our evaluation, we get a kind of secondhand empathy, which does not truly satisfy.

We can avoid gossip by not engaging in it ourselves and responding when other people gossip to us. We can prevent gossip by watching for when we repeat a story about someone else, checking for our motivation, giving ourselves empathy, and then deciding how we want to proceed. When we want to tell someone about a painful interaction we have had, we can recognize that what we need is empathy and find a way to get it, either through self-empathy or by working with someone familiar with NVC. If our need for empathy is met, we will not be drawn to gossip in this way.

It can be more challenging to know how to respond when others gossip to us. We might find ourselves participating only because we don't know how to extract ourselves, or we may participate by default because we don't know what to say in response. Approached through the "right speech" and NVC perspective, we can listen to the intention behind what the person is saying, looking for observations, feelings, and needs. Suppose they gossip about how someone is a jerk for treating them poorly, for example, rather than reinforcing their judgments. In that case, we might ask questions about what the person did that prompted that judgment, and once we've uncovered the observation, we can make guesses as to feelings and needs. I might guess that they are angry and perhaps hurt, and their need for respect was not met. In this way, we help the person get their need for empathy met in a more satisfying way than agreeing with their judgments. If, on the other hand, the person is gossiping to establish shared norms, perhaps telling a story about a coworker, I might guess that they want to meet their need for connection. Whether I make these guesses out loud or simply in my head, in giving empathy, I act in alignment with my value of right speech and satya in providing empathy.

PRACTICING NONVIOLENT COMMUNICATION

Email and telephone

- Choose two or three recent email messages you received. Read through them, looking for observations, feelings, needs, and requests. Write a response that carefully distinguishes those four components, and then rewrite it in more colloquial language, keeping your distinctions clear.
- Before making a phone call, think through what you are requesting of the person and what information they need to want to fulfill that request. Whether you speak to the person directly or leave a voicemail, see how succinctly you can make your request.

Gossip

- Think of a time when you felt drawn to gossip at work. What feelings and needs come up in thinking about it now? What feelings and needs do you think you were acting out of at the time? Notice in your workplace the next time someone engages you in gossip or you overhear gossip. Practice giving silent empathy to the person gossiping.

9

TALKING IN THE WORLD

Those who danced were thought to be quite insane
by those who could not hear the music.
—JOHN MILTON

ON SEPTEMBER 12, 2001, Ike and I had a regularly scheduled NVC practice group at our house. All the regular participants arrived, feeling a wide variety of emotions, including anger, fear, sadness, shock, hurt, and frustration. I was feeling angry about what had occurred the day before, and I stated that I could not begin to understand why it had happened. Our facilitator suggested that Ike play the role of Osama bin Laden, and I was assigned to give bin Laden empathy. As I tried to do this, I focused on guessing the needs bin Laden might have had when he chose the strategy he did for September 11.

The guessed needs that came out—the need for power

and respect for his religion—were needs that I also have. When I realized this, I felt my anger disappearing and instead I felt compassion arising in me. I could connect with another human being on the level of needs, even while I totally disagreed with his actions. Please understand, I believed then and believe now that the strategy Osama bin Laden chose was unacceptable in the extreme and furthermore that he should've been held accountable for that choice by spending the rest of his life in prison. But I found that I could hold that belief *without hating him.*

In fact, I understood that if I hated him, then I was no different than he was for hating my beliefs and culture. Buddha said it best: Hate never dispels hate; only love dispels hate. The irony was that if I hated bin Laden, I was contributing to the very suffering in the world that I said I was so committed to alleviating.

Some years ago, we had a direct experience of how powerful conscious speech can be in the world. One Sunday, Ike and I and a longtime friend were walking toward church in a neighborhood where a number of people were asking passersby for money. One such person approached Ike. This man was as tall as Ike (about six-foot-five) and was acting in a way that we defined as aggressive.

Ike and I had talked many times about what we would do in case something like this happened. So, according to our agreement, I took our friend, a four-foot-ten woman, and myself across the street to safety, so Ike could deal with the man without worrying about us. I quickly turned around to watch what was happening and dialed 911 on my cell phone without pushing "send." While I could not hear any words spoken, I was able to see clearly the body language of both my husband and the man.

The man was leaning in toward Ike, eye to eye, and was asking, I later learned from Ike, for money. Ike often gives money to people on the street, but he remembers that he did not want to give any money to this man, coming as it was from what he interpreted as a "demand" energy. At this point Ike remembered that he had the tool of NVC. He said something like, "I'm feeling afraid with you so close; would be willing to step back?" The man moved back and asked again, with one of his clenched hands thrust forward at about waist level. In response, Ike began to give the man empathy about the "guessed" need to be respected and to be seen and heard. After this second round, the man leaned farther back.

A third request for money was met with more empathy, and this third time the man leaned back even more, so he was standing in the yoga asana Tadasana (Mountain Pose), which is standing with awareness in a perfect vertical line. I observed this alignment and closed my phone, my fear for Ike's safety melting away. When one is centered in Tadasana, there is no aggressive urge; one is fully present.

A fourth round of empathy followed. After Ike gave this empathy, the man leaned over and put his head on Ike's shoulder, with tears in his eyes. Only then did Ike offer the man money. Ike felt he had now "chosen" to give the money and was not being coerced. Thus both Ike's needs and the man's needs appeared to be met at that moment.

The interaction had begun as a potentially violent situation and had ended within a couple of minutes with connection and compassion. This incident cemented in me my dedication to learning and practicing compassionate communication for myself, my family, and the world. Ike and I still remember this incident with gratitude.

CELEBRATING AND MOURNING

One of the most important aspects of using NVC in the world is to learn to mourn with awareness. Too often when we do or say something we later regret, we silently berate ourselves. This energy is not lost; it spills over into the world and into our work.

NVC suggests that when you realize you have done what you don't enjoy or feel that you have contributed to the suffering of another person, that you then mourn in the following way. Give yourself empathy for what you did or said. Use the training wheels process of observations, feelings, and needs. Guess what needs you were trying to meet by the strategy you chose.

Then you may want to address the other person or the group involved in this way: "When I think about what I said yesterday, I feel sad and uncomfortable, because my need to contribute to your well-being (or the well-being of the world) was not met." You may want to add: "I would like to commit now to trying to do it differently next time." As always, follow this statement with a specific request.

This way of stating what is alive in you is not about feeling guilty or punishing yourself. Rather it is about acknowledging what you did and what the consequences were and being willing to try it differently next time. One of the mantras I (Judith) often use after I have mourned in NVC is: How human of me! When I say this to myself, it stimulates me to remember to hold myself with compassion and forgiveness.

On the other hand, we often fail to celebrate our victories, either personally or within our families and groups. Celebrating is such fun. When you want to celebrate with awareness, you might say something like, "When I think about how the decision we made in the meeting turned out, I feel happy, because my needs for cooperation and connection were met." I think it is even better to start your expression with, "I would like to celebrate what just happened." Then offer your observations, feelings, and which needs of yours were met. You will be surprised at how much people enjoy celebrating, as opposed to bragging, and how often people will receive your mourning more deeply than if you had just said, "I'm sorry."

We both believe that mourning and celebrating are crucial components of spreading NVC in the world. Sharing mourning and celebration connects you to others and will soothe your soul when the weight of working for social change becomes too much.

BRINGING AN NVC CONSCIOUSNESS TO THE WORLD

Practicing NVC to effect social change in the world is one of the most challenging ways we can use this communication model. While there is a great need for this work, it can be exhausting and draining in the extreme unless one receives empathy regularly and, we believe, unless one has a regular practice such as meditation or yoga to replenish the body, mind, and soul.

Sometimes we are torn between the conflicting needs to contribute to the world and to protect ourselves from the hurt that we might feel if we fail in our dreams. A story illuminates this predicament. I first heard it in a workshop with Marshall Rosenberg. As I remember it, a man was standing by the bank of a river and noticed a baby floating by. He hurriedly pulled the baby to safety, and as he did, he noticed another and another and another, until the river was full of babies floating by to certain death. He was torn between staying where he was to save as many as he could and instead running upstream to see who was putting all the babies in the river and stopping the process at its root. This illustrates the dilemma many people feel: Do I help the individual next to me in immediate need, or do I work to change the systems that create his suffering in the first place?

While there is no easy answer, our belief is that we can do both. In order to create the kind of world we want to live in and leave to generations to come, we need to help the suffering person who may be near us, beginning with ourselves. Additionally, we need to contribute to changing the beliefs and systems that create that suffering in the first place. However and wherever we decide to spend our energy, our talk and our actions will be more effective if we start with self-awareness. Spiritual speech is a tool for creating this awareness, and as such it offers great hope to us and we hope to you as well.

PRACTICING NONVIOLENT COMMUNICATION

Mourning

- Think about something you said or did in the last couple of weeks that you regret. Mourn it by giving yourself silent empathy for the needs you were trying to meet when you chose the strategy you did. You may need to do this more than once.

- Once you have given yourself empathy, speak to the other person and express your mourning to them. Tell them what you feel when you think about your choices, and then be sure to include the statement that you are committed to doing it differently the next time.

Celebrating

- Think of something you said or did in the last couple of weeks that you want to celebrate. Find a loved one or friend, and state this celebration out loud. Be sure to use observations, feelings, and needs when you do.
- Ask a friend or loved one to share their celebration with you. Help them by giving them empathy for their needs that were met.

RESOURCES

Seek not, my soul, the life of the immortals; but enjoy to the full the resources that are within thy reach.

—PINDAR

JUDITH HANSON LASATER

www.judith.yoga

www.lasater.yoga

www.restorativeyogateachers.com

IKE K. LASATER

https://ikelasater.com

RECOMMENDED READING

Peter Harvey, *An Introduction to Buddhism: Teachings, History, and Practices* (Cambridge, UK: Cambridge University Press, 1990)

Ramamurti S. Mishra, MD, and Shri Brahmananda Sarasvati, *The Textbook of Yoga Psychology: The Definitive Translation and Interpretation of Patanjali's Yoga Sutras* (New York: Baba Bhagavandas Publication Trust, 1997)

Swami Prabhavananda and Christopher Isherwood, *How to Know God: The Yoga Aphorisms of Patanjali* (Hollywood, CA: Vedanta Press, 2007)

Alistair Shearer, *The Yoga Sutras of Patanjali* (New York: Harmony/Bell Tower, 2002)

ORGANIZATIONS

Center for Nonviolent Communication

5600 San Francisco Rd. NE, Suite A
Albuquerque, NM 87109
(505) 244-4041
(505) 247-0414 (fax)
www.cnvc.org

The Center for Nonviolent Communication (CNVC) is a global organization whose vision is a world where all people are meeting their needs and resolving their conflicts peacefully. In this vision, people are using Nonviolent Communication (NVC) to create and participate in networks of worldwide life-serving systems in economics, education, justice, health care, and peace keeping.

The mission of CNVC is to contribute to this vision by facilitating the creation of life-serving systems within ourselves, interpersonally, and within organizations. We do this by living and teaching Nonviolent Communication.

CNVC's aim is to provide ideas, experience, and support for the living of Nonviolent Communication in community. This is accomplished by providing Nonviolent Communication training, materials, organizational consulting, and projects that develop harmonious and effective relationships.

Visit the website for information about books, CDs, and national and international trainings and workshops.

Bay Area Nonviolent Communication
55 Santa Clara Ave., Suite 203
Oakland, CA 94610
(510) 433-0700
(866) 422-9682 (toll free outside the San Francisco Bay Area but within the United States)
(510) 452-3900 (fax)
www.baynvc.org

The mission of Bay Area Nonviolent Communication (BayNVC) is to create a world where everyone's needs matter and people have the skills to make peace. Check the website for workshops and trainings in the San Francisco Bay Area.

ABOUT THE AUTHORS

JUDITH HANSON LASATER

A YOGA TEACHER since 1971, Judith Hanson Lasater holds a bachelor of science degree in physical therapy from the University of California, San Francisco, as well as a doctorate in East–West psychology from the California Institute of Integral Studies. In 1974 she helped found the Institute for Yoga Teacher Education (now the Iyengar Institute of San Francisco), a nationally known yoga teacher training program that has since trained thousands of teachers. In 1975 she cofounded *Yoga Journal* magazine.

Judith modeled yoga poses for *Yoga Journal* and started and served on its editorial advisory board. She created and wrote the asana column in the magazine for thirteen years, as well as dozens of other articles relating to postures, anatomy, kinesiology, yoga therapeutics, breathing exercises, and the psychology and philosophy of yoga. She continues to contribute articles and interviews for *Yoga Journal* as a nationally recognized authority on yoga and serves on the magazine's advisory board.

She is president of the California Yoga Teachers Association, the oldest independent professional yoga teachers' association in the United States.

Judith teaches yoga throughout the world and lives in the San Francisco Bay Area.

IKE K. LASATER

IKE LASATER facilitates the resolution of conflicts, coaches people in conflict, and teaches these skills to others. His mediation work is based on the principles of Nonviolent Communication (NVC), a communication model developed by Marshall Rosenberg, with whom Ike has done most of his formal NVC training. Ike has facilitated NVC and NVC Mediation workshops across the United States and in Australia, Hungry, New Zealand, Pakistan, Poland, and Sri Lanka. He has served as a board member of a number of organizations, including the Center for Nonviolent Communication and the Association for Dispute Resolution of Northern California. He cofounded *Yoga Journal* magazine.

Ike engaged in civil trial practice in the San Francisco financial district for twenty years. He cofounded Banchero

& Lasater, a twenty-person law firm specializing in complex, multiparty, commercial, and environmental cases. He has served as a member of the Mediation Panel for the United States District Court for the Northern District of California since 2001.

Ike is the author of *Words That Work in Business* (PuddleDancer Press). His experience in conflict resolution includes almost four decades of marriage and parenting of three now-adult children (who seem to enjoy interacting with their parents), long-term practice of aikido, Zen meditation, and yoga, and integrating NVC into his daily life since 1996.